The Way of the Innovation Master

The Way of the Innovation Master

Jeffrey Baumgartner

J P B
www.jpb.com
Erps-Kwerps, Belgium

Copyright © 2010 Jeffrey Baumgartner

Published by JPB, an imprint of Bwiti bvba (Belgium)

All rights reserved. Printed in the United States of America. No part of this book may be reproduced in any manner whatsoever without written permission, except in the case of brief quotations embodied in critical articles and reviews. For information, please contact JPB.COM, Diestbrugstraat 45, 3071 Erps-Kwerps, Belgium; email hello@jpb.com or visit www.jpb.com

For my parents, Gerald and Virginia,
without whom not only would this book not be possible,
but I simply would not be.

Contents

Introduction..1

Phase 1: The Plan..5
   Journey: Supertrade...6
   Dialogue: Reacquainting..12
   Lesson: Drafting an Innovation Plan....................................18

Phase 2: The Process..35
   Journey: The Mechanical Chairlift.......................................36
   Dialogue: Robotic Factory Floor..38
   Lesson: The Corporate Innovation Machine.......................41

Phase 3: Motivation..63
   Journey: One Small Step..64
   Dialogue: Not Enough Ideas..67
   Lesson: 12 Ways to Motivate for Creativity........................71
   Lesson: The Three-Cs..78
   Lesson: When the Best Is Not the Best...............................81
   Lesson: Rewarding Innovation...85
   Lesson: Good Rewards for the Wrong People..................89

Phase 4: Ideation..93
   Journey: Bridge Down..94
   Dialogue: Too Many Ideas...96
   Lesson: Creative Problem Solving......................................99
   Lesson: Brainstorming..112
   Lesson: Visual Brainstorming..117
   Lesson: Ideas Campaigns..122
   Lesson: KISS: Keep Ideas Simple, Sweetheart................124
   Lesson: Are Your Ideas Audacious Enough?..................127

Phase 5: Realisation..131
   Journey: Decisions...132
   Dialogue: Decisions, Decisions...135
   Lesson: Evaluation and Implementation...........................139
   Lesson: When to Kill an Idea...150

Lesson: What's Your Plan B?...155
Lesson: Idea Voting Doesn't Work...158
Lesson: Selling Ideas Up the Corporate Ladder..........................164
Lesson: Experimentation 168
Lesson: Concept, Prototype, Production......................................170
Lesson: The Creative Idea Implementation Plan........................172

Phase 6: Culture..179
Journey: A Clear Path Ahead...180
Dialogue: A Much Shorter Journey..184
Lesson: A Dozen Ingredients for a Culture of Innovation 188
Lesson: Prioritising Innovation 195
Lesson: Downsizing the Workforce Downsizes Innovation.....199
Lesson: Glorious Mistakes...203

Phase 7: Arrival 209
Dialogue: Arrival...210
Journey: Arrival...213
Lesson: Departing Thought...215

Acknowledgements..220

Introduction

> **An Innovation Master:** *(n) someone who uses her (or his) knowledge of group creativity and innovation in order to lead an organisation on a journey of growth through the power of its collaborative mind.*

The Way of the Innovation Master is not your typical business book. But, think about it for a moment. Do you really want a book about innovation to be a typical business book? Might a more creative approach to the topic be more suitable? After all, innovation is not a typical business process, which is a big reason why so many managers have trouble getting their heads around the concept. Unlike most other business processes, such as accounting, marketing, product development, innovation is vague, fuzzy and difficult to measure.

Worse, it even involves some actions that the average manager will find less than palatable, actions such as wasting time generating lots of ideas that the company will never use, taking risks and handing big-budget project responsibility to rebellious people. When you look at it this way, it is no wonder so many CEOs proclaim that "Innovation is our number one priority", in order to seem trendy, but avoid actually implementing any real innovation process at all costs. Talking is easier than doing. Or so it may seem.

The problem is that without innovation, companies stagnate, which is not a good thing at all for a business like yours. Meanwhile, if your competitors are adopting innovation processes, they are likely to take the lead in a market you and I know is rightfully yours! Like it or not, then, you will have to adopt an effective innovative process in order to keep your competitors firmly in the rear-view mirror of your corporate vehicle.

And that, my friend, is the whole point of this book. Its aim is to turn you into an Innovation Master so that you can grab your business by the horns and take it down a path of innovation. By so doing you can expect some beneficial side effects, including: increased profitability, improved growth and being a really cool place in which to work.

The Elegance of Threes

The number three permeates the arts. In literature, we have the trilogy. In painting there is the triptych. Architects are taught the rule of three. The very space we live in comprises three dimensions. There is even a theory of cooking which states that the best dishes have three distinct flavours (and, as a side note, if you ever are improvising a dish for a meal, aim for three distinct flavours. It works.).

There is a reason for this preponderance of threes. Three is an elegant and beautiful number. The human mind seems particularly comfortable with sets of three and artists have exploited this fact for centuries.

Now I am exploiting it in this book. The Way of the Innovation Manager is a book of three parallel, yet intertwined cycles which, I hope, will deliver to you all the knowledge and insight you need to become an Innovation Master.

The first cycle is the semi-spiritual journey of Jane, a manager in a large, bureaucratic company that was once an innovative start-up. She must follow the path from her office to the Temple of Ideas, a place where she hopes to study to become an Innovation Master. But, along the way, she will learn subtle lessons about innovation that will help her greatly with her studies.

The second cycle is a dialogue between two old-school company presidents. One has started working with an Innovation Master who is helping him transform his business. The other is only just starting to take an interest in organisational innovation. Both are conservative and find it hard to get their heads around innovation. Nevertheless, through a series of conversations, they both become more more comfortable with innovation and its potential. Their dialogues are vaguely modelled after the dialogues between the gods in Greek drama. But, the company presidents, although powerful, are very human indeed.

The final cycle is a series of straightforward lessons. We start by learning a framework for an innovation plan. We follow that with a structure for organisational innovation. We then work our way through a series of lessons which build upon each other. Many of these lessons, by the way, are based on articles I originally wrote Report 103, an eJournal on business creativity and innovation which you can find at www.jpb.com/report103.

The purpose of this book, of course, is also to take you on a journey from the chair you are sitting in now to the Temple of Ideas where you too will gain the knowledge and insight necessary to become an Innovation Master. Once you have achieved that, your next step will be to take your business on a similar journey.

I hope you and your colleagues will find it a pleasant journey.

Phase 1

The Plan

Journey

Supertrade

Supertrade, the global cash register and business electronics company, was founded in the 1950s in a garage by three creative young engineers fresh out of university. All three came from families in the retail trade and had spent many unhappy hours behind cash registers, managing inventory and doing accounts. They had ideas about how those hours could have been made happier, or at least less tedious, through the use of then modern technology. And they were determined to turn their ideas into reality and from there into a profitable business.

They succeeded admirably. Jack, the wealthiest, put up enough family income to get the business started. His contribution also ensured he became the business's first CEO. Fortunately, he performed this role well in the start-up. Wilbur had a real knack for sales and his family knew a lot of people in the trade, enabling the company to rack up sales quickly. Mike, was shy and quiet but could do incredible things with a set of tools, enabling him to make sexy prototypes of all their concepts. Indeed, Wilbur could often sell dozens of "new" products before they even existed thanks to Mike's prototypes.

The American post-war financial boom sent Americans to the shops, which led to a fabulous growth in the retail industry. That led to more shops, a great many of which purchased Supertrade cash registers and any other business devices the ever growing research and development team could devise. For instance, the firm eventually became a leading producer of barcode scanners.

Throughout its first decade, Supertrade grew through innovation and the opportunities inherent in a growing economy. It expanded into other markets and became a global giant. As luck would have it, Jack's eldest son, Jack Junior, was a wizard with numbers and acquired bachelor's and master's degrees in finance. So, when his father retired, Jack was a natural to take over the company.

He also transformed it from an engineering-oriented firm with tight profit margins to an efficient multinational with bigger margins. And while an increasingly bureaucratic culture stifled innovation, the company expanded by purchasing strategically interesting innovative start-ups and marketing their products better than could their founders. As a result, Supertrade continued to demonstrate slow but steady growth.

However, two things happened at the dawn of the new millennium. Firstly, Jack Junior overestimated the business acumen of his eldest son, who was given the reigns of the firm at just about the same time as the dot-com boom was turning to bust. Jack III, lacked the financial skills of his father and the engineering prowess of his grandfather. Indeed, his only real demonstration of creativity was in the company cars he bought himself, including a slew of Ferraris, and the 'research trips' to Hawaii, Phuket, Bali and the Caribbean. Jack III also had a nasty temper, which struck fear in the hearts of all who worked with him.

Without clear leadership, the company became ever more bureaucratic as managers were reluctant to make decisions that might invoke the wrath of Jack III. At the same time, ever more powerful PC computers, the rise of the Internet and the galloping pace of new technology were changing the face of the retail industry. Supertrade was not keeping up. The company completely failed to see the radio frequency identification (RFID) revolution in retail and missed out on an incredible opportunity. And when it did launch its own products, they were perceived as overpriced and lacking the functionality of more innovative competing products.

With this lack of innovation came reduced income, increasing operational costs and profits that shrank into losses. Competitors out-innovated Supertrade both in implementing new technology in their products as well as streamlining processes for efficiency. As a result, the company had to lay off staff and sell off promising, but unprofitable business units just to survive. It wasn't pretty.

About this time, Jack III learned the hard way that the only thing more dangerous than driving drunk or texting while driving is texting while driving drunk. He wrapped his favourite Ferrari around a telephone pole three times and his last text message was a sad, misspelled status update on Facebook, which remained online for two years after he died. Fortunately, besides Jack, a telephone pole was the only fatality in his pointless and unnecessary accident.

Fortunately, perhaps, Jack III had no children and left such a bad example of management, that it was firmly decided to exclude the offspring of the founders in a search for a new CEO. The board looked at external people and internal people and after much consideration, decided on Jane, a technical genius who had shown remarkable aptitude for people management. She had risen fast in the company and, when invited by the board to present her case for being CEO, knocked their collective socks off with her ideas. Since she would also prove cheaper than hiring from outside and had first-hand knowledge of the many challenges facing Supertrade, it was clear she was an excellent choice. And she was indeed.

Nevertheless, solving the company's myriad problems would not be easy and Jane was not even sure where to start. However she was sure that the solution would involve innovation. There was no other way that Supertrade could not only catch up with, but surpass, competitors. The company had made its name a half century before through innovation. It was time to take that route again. The challenge facing Jane was how she could transform the now bureaucratic giant back into the agile innovator it once was.

An R&D person by profession, Jane did what she did best. She researched. She read books and talked with self-proclaimed experts, of whom she believed there were way too many, the majority having less understanding of organisational innovation than she did!

Fortunately, an intriguing solution presented itself to her before long. In responding to a congratulations note, regarding her promotion, from an ancient, eccentric and brilliant professor of social psychology, Jane explained her situation. She knew the quirky professor would enable her to see her problem in a different light. She was right.

In fact, he wrote to her about the Temple of Ideas: a curious structure of buildings atop an obscure mountain in a South East Asian country not necessarily known for impressive creativity and innovation. The Temple of Ideas was something like the monasteries of long ago. It was a place were creative people could seek refuge to meditate and learn. It was a place where novices in organisational innovation could learn to become Masters of Innovation. It was a place of antiquity and beauty. A place to think, to study, to learn, to grow.

But the Temple of Ideas was unlike a monastery in two key respects. Firstly, it was open to men and women. And secondly, while monasteries are known for strict rules, the Temple of Ideas was more relaxed in that sense. After all, many creative people are rather rebellious.

Sadly, for Jane, the ancient professor did not know – or perhaps he refused to say – where this temple could be found. Indeed, few people knew of its location. For only those both creative and determined enough to find the temple were worthy of becoming Masters of Innovation. Or so she was told.

Jane was inspired and she began her search for the Temple of Ideas. It was not an easy search and it was nearly a year before she identified what she believed to be its location. Then she booked a flight to Bangkok, arranged for a chartered aeroplane, a Range Rover and a guide to get her to the mountain.

* * *

As it happens, I was in the gatehouse at the foot of the mountain when Jane arrived, dishevelled, hot and tired. "Do you know the Temple of Ideas?" she asked of me.

"Indeed, I do," I happily informed her. "But tell me, please, why you are looking for the temple."

"Why should I do that?" she asked eyeing me more carefully.

"Because I am the temple's gatekeeper today," I explained.

Satisfied, she told me the story of Supertrade Industries and of her desire to become an innovation master so she could transform the company from being a dim example of mediocrity to being a shining example of corporate innovation.

"Ah, yes. You definitely want the Temple of Ideas. It is there, at the top of the mountain," I said pointing. "I will take you there."

"That's not necessary," she said. "I have climbing experience. I can get there myself."

"I'm sure you have and you could," I said. "But it is necessary and a part of the learning process."

"Oh, are you an Innovation Master?" she asked.

"Perhaps. I have much to learn," I answered. Then I changed the subject. "It's late in the afternoon. We can start early tomorrow morning. It will be a new day with many possibilities open to us. Do you have a room in town, or can we put you up here for the night?"

"I have a room in town," she replied as she glanced inside. The gatehouse is an attractive, creatively decorated old building, if I may say so myself. I suspect she would have liked to have stayed there.

"Very good," I said. "I will meet you here at dawn."

"Great," she replied. We shook hands formally and she walked away.

Appearing out of the early morning mist she arrived, decked out in appropriate climbing clothes and a designer rucksack on her back. I invited her into the gatehouse and spread out on the table a map. It displayed the myriad possibilities for getting to the top of a mountain littered with stairways, chairlifts, ladders, rock faces and much more. However, there was no clear path to the top and it was obvious we would have to use a variety of means to get to the temple of ideas.

"Oh my, there is a lot here," she remarked. "Is this like a maze with just one path to the Temple of Ideas?"

"No, don't worry. There are many paths to the top. And you can even change your path as you climb. But it is wise to start with a plan. Otherwise, you could easily find yourself not achieving your goal. Now, how would you like to do this?"

Jane opted for a route that combined efficiency with some pleasant walking and fine views. We noted her route on the map, pocketed it and walked through an elegant, very old stone gate to a long flight of stairs. We began climbing as the mist started to clear. I could just make out the Temple of Ideas at the top of the mountain. It is always good when your goal is in sight.

It was indeed going to be a good day.

Dialogue

Reacquainting

Some distance from the same mountain, the one upon which the Temple of Ideas stands, is a luxury hotel. Its air-conditioned, carpeted interior is a world apart from the hot Asian countryside outside. On the top floor is a lounge with picture windows looking out in all directions. From the west-facing window, the mountain in question can be seen.

Inside the lounge, two men stand. Their worn faces and grey hair suggests they are in their late 50s or early 60s. Their accents and manners are distinctly well-bred, well-educated British. In fact, they both run family companies that have been around in one form or another for generations.

One company president opens a bottle of fine 2000 Bordeaux and pours the other a drink as they stand in air-conditioned comfort.

Alpha: I haven't seen you in ages, my old friend. The rumour mill says you've been on some kind of spiritual thingie or another.

Beta: More of another, really. I've been back and forth to the Temple of Ideas. It's quite near here. Do you know it?

Alpha: Don't think so. Is that some sort of artist retreat or meditation centre or somesuch? Great place to meet the opposite sex, I expect...

Beta:	No, no. It's a place for senior management types, like us, who want to become Innovation Masters.
Alpha:	A what!? Is that anything like a Hare Krishna?
Beta:	No, of course not.
Alpha:	You won't be giving out pamphlets at airports and that sort of thing now, will you?
Beta:	Don't be silly! Let me explain.
Alpha:	Because I'm not sure I could take such a pamphlet, even from an old school chum, like you. I'd have to refuse, you know.
Beta:	Calm down, man. It's nothing of the sort. An Innovation Master is simply someone who knows a thing or three about innovation in organisations.
Alpha:	Oh, "innovation master". I misheard you. So, you reckon this innovation stuff is worth getting one's head around, do you? It isn't just a fad then?
Beta:	No. It's more than that. Otherwise, I wouldn't be climbing mountains and going to temples, now would I?
Alpha:	No, I suppose you wouldn't.
Beta:	Of course not!
Alpha:	Well, we're keen on innovation at the office as well. Indeed, I've just done an interview with some American business magazine. Told the interviewer that "innovation is our company's number one priority."

Beta: Really now? And is it?

Alpha: Between you and me and these wine glasses, profit is our number one priority. But I reckon we've got to make the right noise about innovation to please the shareholders and all.

Beta: Absolutely. But as the Americans say, perhaps you need to walk the walk as well as talk the talk. [tops up Alpha's glass with more wine] Are you walking the walk?

Alpha: Yes, yes. Of course. I've just sent a memo around to the employees telling them about this innovation thing and telling them that they'd bloody well better start innovating, you know.

Beta: Really?

Alpha: Oh yes, but not in those words, of course.

Beta: Of course not.

Alpha: I say, this is a marvellous Bordeaux.

Beta: Isn't it, though? It's a Château Giscours 2000. When I saw it on the wine list, I had to order a bottle.

Alpha: Well done! You always have had an eye for an excellent bottle.

Beta: Getting back to this innovation thing, I'm not sure you can simply tell your people to be innovative and then expect them to innovate, you know.

Alpha: Of course not, old stick. I told them to have ideas as well.

Beta:	Really, and what should they do with their ideas?
Alpha:	Why innovate of course!
Beta:	I'm not sure that's good enough.
Alpha:	What do you mean?
Beta:	Well, you can't just tell people to be profitable, now can you?
Alpha:	No, but that's different.
Beta:	Is it? I rather thought innovation was about improving the old bottom line.
Alpha:	Well, yes, I suppose it is.
	And you? What are you and your people doing about innovation in your biz?
Beta:	Right now, we're doing an innovation plan. My Innovation Master at the temple, a jolly clever girl she is, made it clear it wasn't enough just to waffle on about innovation. Says we actually have to draw up a plan and follow it. She's even given us a nifty template to use.
Alpha:	Indeed?
Beta:	Oh yes. I've even flown her our to HQ so she and our managers can go though her worksheet. It's full of clever questions that have been keeping the old managers busy the past few weeks.

Alpha: That doesn't sound very productive to me, old boy. Are you sure you're not wasting time with one of those fads like re-engineering or chaos theory?

Beta: I believe chaos theory was more about maths and physics.

Alpha: Oh! Well, no wonder it didn't work for us.

Beta: Anyway, the innovation team has drawn up a rather clever plan. It actually makes a lot of sense. We're going to give it a go.

Alpha: Marvellous. So you reckon she's good, this Innovation Master?

Beta: Seems to know her stuff awfully well.

Alpha: Do you think you might send her round to our HQ when you're done with her, then?

Beta: I'd love to, old bean. But she's not like a consultant who flies out, fixes things and invoices you out of your shirt. You've got to work out where the Temple of Ideas is located and then make the journey there. It's quite a journey!

Alpha: Oh dear, I'm not sure that's my cup of tea. I can barely work out The Times' crossword, you know. Perhaps I can have my secretary work it out. She's a clever ducky at that kind of thing, you know. Practically runs the business, she does.

Meanwhile, how about another glass of that phenomenal Bordeaux if you don't mind?

Beta: Of course. Here you go.

Alpha: Thanks awfully. Now, tell me all about your innovation plan.

Beta: I'm afraid I can't. You'll have to read the next chapter instead.

Alpha: Well, if I must.

Beta: You must. But you won't regret it.

Lesson

Drafting an Innovation Plan

The first phase in your journey to becoming an Innovation Master and turning your company into an innovation-driven organisation is to devise an innovation plan. It is not enough simply to say "innovation is our number one priority" or to demand that your managers become more innovative. Sorry.

Rather, you need to plot out a plan for innovation that starts with strategy and works its way through idea generation, evaluation, implementation and profit. And, frankly, it's that last item that makes innovation worth all the trouble. If your company is successful in finding, developing and implementing innovative ideas, it will realise the benefits through reduced operational costs and increased income which, it goes without saying, is excellent for your bottom line!

This is the innovation plan that the Innovation Masters at the Temple of Ideas first assign to their novices. I will assign it to Jane. Beta's Innovation Master assigned it to him. Now it's your turn.

A) Innovation Goals

What are Your Innovation Goals?
Before you can go anywhere with your innovation planning, you need to identify your innovation goals. You should have one primary innovation goal which will be closely tied with, if not identical to, your corporate strategy. It should also reflect how your customers identify you

and your brand. For instance, until recently, Toyota's primary innovation goal was to build quality cars efficiently. And their cars have been recognised as being reliable and well-built. Apple's primary innovation goal is currently to bring out very stylish rethinks of popular technology gadgetry, such as music players, mobile telephones and tablet computers. Again, this is how the public recognises them.

In addition, you will probably have two or three secondary innovation goals. These are not always so obvious to customers, but are important to maintaining a competitive lead. Sometimes, they are directly related to your primary innovation goal. One of Toyota's secondary goals has been to make as efficient as possible the delivery of parts to their assembly plants. This keeps inventory low, keeps costs low (no paying for parts they will not need for a long time) and involves suppliers more closely with production.

Individual business units and departments in your company may also have their own innovation goals relating to their responsibilities. It is important that these goals align with corporate goals.

Innovation goals should be open-ended so that your company can always strive to improve itself with respect to the goal. Thus, to build the most technically-advanced widgets on the market is an admirable innovation goal. To develop a widget that meets a specific specification, on the other hand, is not an innovation goal. It may be a short term goal, but it cannot be your primary innovation goal.

Tasks for you:

- List your primary innovation goal.
- List your secondary innovation goals (if any).
- (Optional) list innovation goals of main business units and/or departments (alternatively, pass this document to the heads of each unit for completion).

Where Can You Find Insights?

In order to innovate towards your goals, you need insights. Insights are sources of information, intelligence and inspiration that inspire ideas that move you towards achieving your innovation goals. Insights may include trade journals or technical magazines that keep you and your colleagues abreast of latest developments in the field. They may include visiting customers' facilities in order to understand better their needs.

Sources of insight will include the obvious, such as journals, trade shows and market research. But they should also include less obvious places to seek insight. Bear in mind your competitors are also using the same obvious places to seek insight. Hence, these insights are more likely to produce incremental innovation rather than breakthrough innovation.

Less obvious sources of insight might include visits to the local art galleries, looking at the operations of completely unrelated industries, attending trade shows in fields not your own, reading news magazines and so on.

You will be asked below to list existing sources of insight as well as potential sources of insight. In order to identify potential sources of insight, we recommend a little brainstorming. Spend some time thinking about all the potential sources of inspiration that might exist in this world and list them on a sheet of paper. It doesn't matter how ludicrous your ideas are. List them. If at first your idea does not seem ridiculous, it is probably not very creative!

If you are working with a team, each member of the team should write down their ideas. Then compile a grand list of everyone's ideas. Then let people add more ideas that may have been inspired by the existing ideas.

If you are not rushed, wait 24 hours and then follow up with another short idea generation period. Again, compile all ideas onto the master list.

Once the idea generation is complete, and only then, go through all the ideas with the team. Give every idea a score of 0-5 points for its relevance to your goals; and 0-5 points for its potential to inspire outrageous ideas. Every idea that gets five or more total points should be put on the list of potential insights.

> Tasks for you:
> - Make a list of your existing sources of insight for your primary innovation goals.
> - Make a list of potential sources of insight for your primary innovation goals.
> - For each of your secondary innovation goals, make a list of existing sources of insight.
> - For each of your secondary innovation goals, make a list of potential sources of insight (Note: too much brainstorming in one go doesn't work. Best to divide this task between teams or to take breaks between sessions.)

Evaluation Criteria

One of the consequences of preparing and putting into action this innovation plan is that you will start seeing a lot more ideas rolling in. In order to filter these, you will need evaluation criteria which you can use to identify which ideas should be taken to the next stage, which ideas need to be improved to meet criteria and which ideas are best forgotten.

We find that about five criteria per category are ideal. But fewer or, in some cases, more are also good. Be careful, however, about having too many evaluation criteria. This could prove a stumbling block against implementing ideas.

We recommend that criteria should be matters of degree rather than absolute. Hence, "Should be cost effective to manufacture" or "How inexpensive will this idea be to manufacture?" are better than, "Should cost no more than €50 per unit to manufacture." With absolute measures, there is a danger that a fantastic idea is thrown out because it falls slightly short of an arbitrary metric.

Finally, bear in mind that the initial evaluation simply identifies ideas that should be taken seriously and developed further. It will not obligate you to invest millions in seemingly strange ideas!

> Task for you:
> - For each innovation goal, list three to five evaluation criteria for measuring its viability.

Idea Realisation Process

If an idea gets a good evaluation, it should be put on track for implementation. This may include market research, writing a business case, building a prototype and similar actions. Ideas that involve substantial investment, such as developing new products, will normally involve several actions between evaluation and implementation. Low investment ideas may go directly to implementation.

Bear in mind that potential breakthrough innovations will likely be very different to the kinds of ideas that you typically process. Hence you should be sure that idea realisation processes have the flexibility to take on radical ideas.

> Task for you:
> - For each innovation goal, list the typical actions that should be taken in order to realise an idea.

B) Barriers

Barriers to Innovation in Your Firm

Every company has barriers to innovation: people, tools and/or processes that prevent employees from innovating. Think not only about barriers to innovative ideas suggested by upper management. More importantly, think about the factory worker on the floor who has a fantastic idea about reducing wastage on the assembly line. Imagine this idea could slash production costs by 5%. What barriers would prevent her idea from reaching the senior managers who would need to authorise its implementation?

In my experience, the most frequently cited barrier to innovation is middle managers. This is a tragedy. Middle managers should facilitate innovation by motivating their subordinates to think more creatively (innovative implementations are born of creative ideas) and selling those ideas to top management. However, all too often middle managers tend to discourage ideas of their subordinates because they don't like change, they are afraid subordinates' ideas will make them look bad or they know their managers will kill ideas.

Other barriers to innovation include absurd processes, too many approval committees, bureaucratic procedures and fear of risks associated with innovation, for example: reprimand or worse if an idea does not produce good results.

> Task for you:
> - List the barriers to innovation in your company.

Overcoming Barriers to Innovation

Barriers can be broken down, climbed over, jumped over, passed around or blown to smithereens. For each of the listed barriers to innovation, you will need to find one or more methods for overcoming it. Sometimes the solutions will be obvious. At other times you will need to brainstorm (see above), do research to identify how others have overcome similar barriers or ask outside experts.

You can use the brainstorming technique described in section 2 above, but rate each idea on how potentially effective it might be, with zero points for not at all effective and five points for very effective.

> Task for you:
> - For each barrier you have listed, list actions to be taken to overcome that barrier.

C) Managing Innovative Risk

The innovation process is fraught with risk. Even during the initial creative phase of having ideas and sharing them with management, there is risk.

Risk and Creative Ideas

In many organisations, people sharing ideas, particularly outrageous ideas, may face ridicule. In companies that are particularly unwelcoming to change, people who frequently suggest new ideas are branded as trouble-makers. However, you should bear in mind that the more creative an idea is, the more outrageous it initially sounds. If your employees are afraid to share their more outrageous ideas, your company loses out on their most creative ideas!

Your company needs to have a welcoming environment where crazy ideas are rewarded and people who suggest them are challenged to turn their ideas into viable concepts. Managers and team leaders in many companies have a tendency to reject new ideas immediately, with phrases like "we have no budget for that", "[some senior manager or committee] will never approve that" or "don't be ridiculous!" They need to learn instead to compliment new ideas and then challenge (see Three Cs chapter).

Tasks for you:

- How well are outrageous and unusual ideas welcomed in your company?
- How do employees feel about sharing ideas with colleagues and managers?
- How do employees feel about participating in brainstorming and similar events in your company?

We recommend you get feedback from employees, ideally through a third party or questionnaire that allows anonymity. Often top management and people towards the bottom of the corporate ladder have a different notion of this issue!

Risk and Innovative Projects

Further along the innovation process, at the implementation stage, risk is also a factor. Ideas with high innovation potential, in particular, are by their nature new and different to the usual products and processes. If a high risk idea succeeds, the pay-off is likely to be substantial. But if it fails, the costs can also be substantial. If your company punishes failure, individuals and teams will be reluctant to involve themselves in potentially risky projects. At the same time, if a project is showing poor results, those in charge will be reluctant to bail out of the project for fear of the consequences. As a result, they will throw more resources into a failing project in hopes of saving it. Thus, if and when the project does fail, the costs are much higher than if the project had been killed, or at least thoroughly reviewed, at an early stage.

The enlightened innovative company recognises this problem and ideally celebrates failure. Teams responsible for projects that do not succeed are rewarded for their efforts and some kind of debriefing action is performed in order to disseminate information about why the project failed. While failing once at a particular project should be considered a valuable learning experience, failing several times with the same concept is not good! Hence the need for debriefing.

Nevertheless, every company has a comfort zone with respect to risk. Projects within that comfort zone are more likely to be authorised than those that extend outside that zone. You should define as much as possible the comfort zone. This will enable teams to propose projects that exist within the zone and are therefore more likely to be approved.

It is generally wise to launch innovative projects with a series of milestones at which the project is reviewed. If it has not achieved the expected results at each milestone, the project should be cancelled unless there is a good reason for not meeting expectations. Such milestones help ensure that a failing project is not excessively costly to the company and allows the creative people managing it to tackle a new project which may bring better results. Moreover, such milestones often make it easier to sell projects to senior managers.

Tasks for you:

- When a project fails, what happens to the individuals involved? What is the best case scenario? What is the worst case scenario?

- How do people in your company feel about getting involved in an innovative, yet risky project: excited by the opportunity or frightened by the opportunity or somewhere in the middle? Why?

- How should you deal with potentially innovative projects that fail?

- How might you ensure that others in the company learn from the mistakes of a failed project?

- How might you motivate people to kill poorly performing projects before they drain too much budget?

- For each innovation goal, how might you structure a process to kill projects and learn from the mistakes?

- For each of your innovation goals, describe the comfort zone for projects.

D) Motivation

Motivating People to Participate

One of the challenges you will face with your innovation process is motivating people to participate. There are two reasons for this. Firstly, participants in your innovation process need to know about activities, tools and expectations. Even with the best tools in the world, if people do not know about your initiative, they cannot participate. You need to create an innovation communication plan to deal with this challenge.

Secondly, and more challenging, is motivating reluctant employees to share ideas and get involved in innovative projects. At the idea generation stage, a commonly heard complaint is: "I don't have time to participate in this." Indeed, in a survey carried out by Wayne Morris and published by jpb.com, the number one barrier to organisational creativity was cited as time.

But, your employees most likely spend at least 35 hours per week working for you. Clearly, the problem is not time so much as priorities. Many people simply do not feel that participating in idea generation and development activities is sufficiently important to make time. They see other daily tasks as being more critical.

Thus, on one hand, you need to demonstrate to employees the importance of innovation in your company. This should be part of your communication plan. On the other hand, you need to motivate people to participate in innovation-related activities. You can do this in part by giving rewards for participation.

However, rewards are far more complex than many people realise. In a nutshell, small rewards are better than big rewards (you can always promote someone who consistently provides innovative ideas – without tying the promotion exclusively to idea generation). Moreover, rewards should be tied to participation and creativity and never to "best ideas".

In addition, rewarding teams rather than individuals is very effective for promoting collaboration. If the entire team is rewarded for ideas, they have reason to collaborate. If only individuals are rewarded, team members have reason to keep their best ideas to themselves – especially if the rewards are substantial.

Finally, responsibility is a great reward. Putting the individual or team responsible for a great idea in charge of developing that idea is a fine reward that recognises creativity, talent and skills.

> Tasks for you:
>
> - Outline a communication plan for your innovation process. Indicate what media you will use, how it will be used and how often. Who will be in charge?
>
> - Outline a reward plan. What kind of rewards will you provide, to whom and on what basis? Will you offer a consistent reward scheme or will it vary from event to event?

E) Processes

Idea Generation Actions

What kind of idea generation actions do you envision using in your company? Actions include brainstorming, ideas campaigns, suggestion schemes, focus groups, customer feedback and actions which provide insight (see item 2 "Where can you find insights" above). When thinking about actions, bear in mind your innovation goals and work with actions that facilitate working towards those goals. Suggestion schemes, for instance, do not give you much if any control over the direction and theme of idea generation. If your aim is to produce cutting edge technology, you will want to be careful about how you use customer feedback as most of your customers will probably not be up to date on the latest research in your area. Henry Ford famously said that if he had asked his customers what they wanted, they would have told him they wanted faster horses!

In addition to the actions, think also about the people who will participate in those actions. Employees are obvious for inclusion. But consider also working with suppliers, customers and possibly even the public. Many companies we have worked with have involved suppliers in their idea generation activities with great success. Some thought can also be given about whether to focus idea generation in small teams or open all challenges to everyone. In most cases, you will want something in the middle.

If you expect the bulk of idea generation to go on within teams, bear in mind that the best results come from diverse teams, that is teams that include people with different backgrounds, training and experience. Diversity of culture can bring substantial range of thinking – so if your company has people from different countries, include cultural diversity in teams as well.

See the Lesson on Creative Problem Solving (CPS) for more detailed information on idea generation methods.

> Tasks for you:
> - What idea generation activities do you currently use, if any?
> - For each of these, what kind of results have you seen? If poor, why? How might you improve results?
> - What other idea generation activities might you investigate? How would you use them?

Innovation Tools

There are a lot of innovation tools, particularly software, on the market today. Software exists to support mind-mapping, brainstorming, idea management and innovation process management. In addition, web-based collaboration tools such as Blogs and Wikis can be used effectively by small companies. For instance, teams can collaborate to develop ideas in Wikis.

As noted above, before investing in innovation software, be sure that it supports your innovation plan. It is also worth bearing in mind how software is to be used. Mind-maps are great for individuals and small teams, but not at all effective for large idea generation initiatives. Also, some people simply do not like working with mind-maps and forcing them to do so would be detrimental to their creative thinking skills.

Although most innovation tools are software products, some are not. Providing everyone in your company with small notebooks for writing down ideas can be a highly effective tool. A conference room with lots of whiteboard space can facilitate ideation sessions. A comfortable room with lots of toys, building blocks, paper and other media can be great for creative thinking.

Tasks for you:

- What innovation tools, if any, are you currently using or have you recently been using?
- What results have you experienced with these tools? How might you improve the results?
- What additional tools might you consider using? How?

F) People

Responsibilities

An individual, a team or a group of individuals should be put in charge of overseeing and monitoring your innovation plan. You should identify not only the individuals who will take on these responsibilities to start with, but also the profile of people who will take over should one or more of those responsible leave the organisation or be moved to another area of the company. On the other hand, if you intend to hire an innovation manager, draw up a description of skills, training and experience you would expect from an innovation manager. In a smaller company, it may make more sense to work with a part time consultant who can initially oversee your innovation process.

You may wish to centralise innovation to one team or individual (in a smaller company), or you may wish to have an innovation person in every business unit, each of whom is coordinating with a central innovation person/team.

Tasks for you:

- Who will take charge of the innovation plan initially? (Use a job description if you intend to hire someone for this position).
- If the individual(s) above can no longer support the innovation team, from where will replacements be found?
- How will you structure innovation personnel across your company?

Involving Outsiders (Open Innovation)

Open innovation is a new trend that involves bring outsiders into your innovation process. Open innovation encompasses everything from inviting a few suppliers to collaborate on ideas to public suggestion schemes that allow anyone to submit ideas to your organisation.

If your company works with a lot of suppliers, it is almost certainly within your best interest to invite suppliers to participate in the innovation process from idea development to evaluation to implementation.

Public suggestion schemes, while high in profile, are of questionable value, particularly as most tools that provide this service do not align idea generation with your innovation plan. They also require a substantial amount of work if every submitted idea is to be reviewed.

On the other hand, tools that invite outsiders to submit solutions to focused challenges can be quite effective and good results have been seen. The advantage to such tools is that you pose the challenges to ensure they are a part of your innovation plan. Moreover, ideas can be evaluated according to the criteria you set.

When involving outsiders in your innovation process, be sure to consider intellectual property rights issues. It should be clear from the outset who owns any patents or other intellectual property associated with ideas submitted to your company. We recommend involving a legal expert to advise on this issue prior to involving outsiders.

Tasks for you:

- What groups of people might you involve in your innovation initiative, and how?
- What methods and tools might you use to support their involvement? (brainstorming, ideas campaigns, innovation process management, etc.).

G) Review and Everything Else

Reviewing the Plan

Your innovation plan should be dynamic and evolving over time. You will gain experience, the market will change and disruptions might drastically alter your market. You should review your innovation process regularly and modify it according to new needs.

> Tasks for you:
> - How will you review your innovation plan?
> - What metrics, if any, will you use? How will you collect the data?
> - Who will be responsible for the review?
> - How often will formal reviews take place?

Everything Else

Every company has its own special needs. If there are other elements that should be included in your innovation plan, include them here.

> Last task for you
> - Are there any other issues you wish to include in your innovation plan? If so, list them here.

Phase 2
The Process

Journey

The Mechanical Chairlift

The stairway ended in a large, stone platform on the side of the mountain. We stopped and admired the view. Jane was impressed. "I can see so clearly from here," she said. "And even the neighbouring villages."

"Indeed, and we have only just begun. Here, look at this." I said pointing to a model of the mountain on a table in the centre of the platform. On it, we could see the various ways to the top of the mountain, complete with small models. A yellow smiley marked our current "You are here" location, a short way up the mountain. At the top of the model stood a replica of the Temple of Ideas.

"You can see what we have done and what we have yet to do more clearly on this model than you can on the map," I remarked as we both studied the model.

"Well, we haven't really covered much ground yet," Jane observed. "But the journey does seem more doable now that we've got a solid start. And this model makes the route so clear."

"Indeed," said I. Then I pointed to the right of the smiley. "Here is where we start the next part of our climb. Are you ready?"

"Yes," she said.

We left the platform by a wooden gate and followed a dirt path. After ten minutes or so, we could hear a faint, continuous roar in the background. As we continued it picked up in volume until we came round a bend and could see the waterfall that was providing the background noise.

More apparent, on either side of the waterfall, a large scaffold like structure was bolted into the mountainside. Between the two scaffolds ran an axle holding a waterwheel, of which about one third was inside the waterfall. The wheel spun surprisingly quickly. On our side of the waterfall, the axle ended in a large gearwheel which was connected by a chain to another gearwheel which, in turn was connected to a set of chains, gearwheels and axles that ran to a final large gearwheel connected to a cable going up the mountain. Hanging from the cable were a number of ornate, iron benches. This unusual chairlift was moving slowly and steadily up the mountain on one side and down the other.

"That's quite a machine!" she remarked.

"Thanks! We are proud of it," I said. "You know, it's powered solely by the waterfall."

"Really?" she asked examining the system carefully. "I am impressed!"

"Thanks again," I replied. Now let's try it out."

We climbed onto a bench and rode the chairlift up the mountainside. The machine creaked and groaned and the benches swayed gently in the wind. But the ornate seats, the mechanical sounds against the background roar of the waterfall and the stunning view was aesthetically overpowering, preventing either of us from worrying about any potential accidents from the odd chairlift.

Dialogue

Robotic Factory Floor

The two company presidents walk along a factory floor somewhere in rural Japan. Only a scant few workers can be seen as the factory has largely been automated by computers and robots. A quiet hum of efficient machinery hums in the background.

Alpha: Fascinating place this. Hardly a labourer about anywhere. And look at these machines. Shine like they're new. Only the Japanese can keep things so neat.

Beta: Indeed. I love this place.

Alpha: I can see that. But why did you ask me to come here?

Beta: I'm thinking of buying the company.

Alpha: Ah. I see. It would be a nice complement to your existing businesses, wouldn't it?

Beta: Indeed.

The CEOs walk along quietly for a moment while watching how bits and pieces get put together into products and dropped into packaging by tireless robots.

Beta: I say, have you ever done anything with that Innovation Planning thing I gave you?

Alpha: Yes actually. Our R and D director absolutely jumped on it when I told her about it. Said it was what the company has been needing since around the dawn of mankind or thereabouts. Not sure I approve of her attitude sometimes, but she's a jolly good R and D lass.

Beta: And? How is it progressing?

Alpha: Got a bang of a start and all that. Diane, the R and D lass, brought in a couple of other directors and had a real go at it. Gave me a PowerPoint summary and all. Seems like good stuff. But...

Beta: But?

Alpha: Like I say, Diane and the team have done up a nifty document and are rather excited. But some of the older chaps are concerned that it's a lot of change for not much value.

Beta: Oh dear. But you intend to implement it, don't you?

Alpha: I suppose we really ought to. They've put a lot of time and effort into it.

Beta: I believe you ought to. You know, my Innovation Master at the Temple of Ideas.

Alpha: Her again? You've got a thing about her, don't you?

Beta: Well, she's jolly clever and has helped me really get my head around organisational innovation and all that.

Alpha: And is she a good-looker?

Beta: [laughs] You know, she told me that when one gets one's innovation process up and running, it's rather like a machine.

Alpha: Is that so?

Beta: It is so. She reckons it will just hum along like this network of machines here [waves his arm in the air as if presenting the robots around the factory].

Alpha: [thinks for a moment] How does she reckon that?

Beta: Read on, old sport, and all will become clear.

Alpha: Ok.

Lesson

The Corporate Innovation Machine

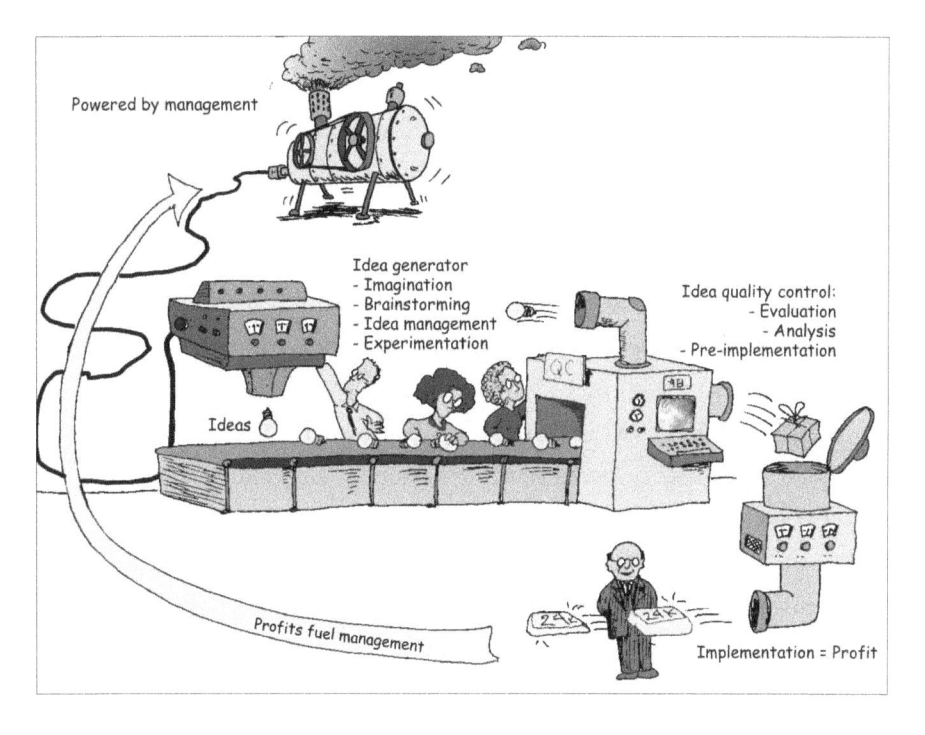

The waterfall powered chairlift that Jane and I rode upon and the robot-filled factory floor which Alpha and Beta visited are both essentially closed machines comprised of smaller machines. Likewise, the corporate innovation process can be viewed as a machine comprising several smaller machines or sub-processes within the overall process. When all of the machines work properly and connect to their fellow machines, the system runs smoothly and indefinitely. Let's see how it works.

Powered by Management

The corporate innovation machine is powered by management. Just as the most sophisticated machine will not run without a power source, likewise your corporate innovation strategy will go nowhere without top management taking the lead.

As a senior manager, your main task is to create within the organisation a culture of innovation which will empower workers to think creatively, collaborate on ideas and contribute their ideas to the company. This is not an easy task, but done well it will make construction of the remainder of the innovation machine a relatively easy job.

Senior Management Must Do a Few Things

First and foremost, you must take the lead with innovation. If you talk about the importance of innovation, but neither you nor any member of the C-level management team is seen to be involved in the actual process, it sends a very strong message to your employees: top brass does not take this innovation thing seriously. So, take it seriously and take the lead!

The next step is to prepare an innovation plan. Without a plan, any innovation initiative is doomed to failure! And preparation of this plan must be overseen by management. After all, an innovation plan should be aligned with strategy.

Also critical for management is to ensure that there is an environment of trust. If the workforce does not trust the company, they will not innovate for the company. Survey after survey has shown that trust is one of the most critical factors in establishing a culture of innovation. If your workforce trusts the company, this is not an issue. If not, establishing trust must be your very first step.

One of the major stumbling blocks to any innovation initiative is creative risk. And this is something you need to address in order to ensure the initiative works. For many people, sharing a potentially absurd idea with their company is overly risky. At best, they may be ridiculed by their colleagues. At worst, they may be reprimanded by their superiors or even damage their career progression ("Jerry's not really management material. He keeps coming up with those absurd ideas that are completely impractical"). If the level of creative risk in your organisation is too high, people will keep ideas to themselves, rather than share them. You need to ensure creative risk is as low as possible.

You will also need to establish a rewards scheme. Rewarding innovative thinking is an important part of an idea management-based innovation strategy. Rewards increase motivation for employees to continue developing and sharing ideas. There are various methods of rewarding ideas. Some companies favour public recognition through newsletters, intranet sites and meetings. Some offer work related benefits such as additional time off or attending overseas conferences. And some give small gifts such as electronic gadgets, coupons for local shops or chocolates. Whatever system you choose, it should be perceived as consistent and fair. Management should not offer substantial cash rewards for ideas. These inevitably lead to greed and perceived unfairness.

Last, but not least, you need to implement creative ideas. Ideas are no more than ideas until they are implemented. Management needs to take charge of implementing creative ideas so that they may become innovations which deliver value to the company. Highly creative ideas, which have the potential to become breakthrough innovations are also highly risky. Thus management must establish procedures for implementing such ideas, usually together with a set of milestones against which progress of the idea's development can be monitored and decisions made as whether or not the implementation should go on.

How management implements these actions varies from organisation to organisation and depends on existing culture, existing tools, innovation goals and facilities.

Idea Generator

If management is the power source of the innovation machine, then the idea generator – the tools and techniques for generating ideas – is the motor that drives the innovation process.

Principles

Before we look at idea-generation tools, it is important to look at the key terms and concepts relevant to organisational creativity and innovation.

Creativity versus Innovation

In the business world, the terms, "creativity" and "innovation" are often used interchangeably. They should not be and it is important to understand the difference.

> *Creativity* is the generation of new ideas by combining existing ideas and concepts in new ways
>
> *Innovation* is the implementation of creative ideas in order to generate value, usually through reduced operational costs, increased income or both.

Individual Creativity Versus Organisational Creativity

Individual creativity is, of course, the creativity of an individual person. People can learn to be more creative by reading books, participating in workshops, learning creative thinking techniques and so on. Organisational creativity is the creativity of an organisation. Unlike people, however, organisations cannot simply pick up a book and learn to be more creative. Likewise, even if an organisation is full of creative people (and most are), that does not necessarily make the organisation more creative.

Making an organisation more creative and more innovative is much more complex, requiring the establishment of a culture of innovation together with tools for creative collaboration; in other words: implementing a strategy along the lines of the innovation machine strategy.

Creative Collaboration
Collaboration is an essential element of organisational innovation. When a team of people come together to devise and develop ideas, they can potentially be much more innovative than any individual member of the team can be on her own.

However, to be effective, teams must be comprised of a variety of people with different backgrounds and areas of expertise. In a corporate setting this requires, at minimum, that teams are made up of people from different divisions within the company. At best, those people will also come from different locations or countries. As a rule of thumb: a greater variety of people participating in the idea generation process equals a higher level of creativity and innovation.

Creative collaboration occurs in several ways:

- Creative teams put together by management in order to handle a specific task or project. When management puts together such a team, an effort should always be made to build the team with people from different divisions and locations. People new to the company can be particularly valuable team members as they will bring to the team fresh thinking unprejudiced by established corporate notions.

- Creative teams that are formed when an employee asks one or more colleagues to assist her with a task. Unfortunately, when people form their own teams, they tend to work with other people in their own division and with whom they have worked in the past. This is not ideal for creative thinking. As much as possible, employees should be encouraged to form teams with members of other departments. An on-line staff directory or knowledge map can help considerably for finding team members with specific areas of expertise.

- Brainstorming groups that are brought together to perform a single brainstorming session (see below). Again, an effort should be made to bring as wide a variety of people as possible into each brainstorming session. When appropriate, business partners, customers and others from outside the company should be brought in to participate.

- Networking that employees do when they seek the assistance of a colleague for ideas, advice or help. Networking tools, such as staff directories and discussion forum tools can help encourage people to network outside their departments and immediate contacts.

- Open collaboration that is possible through web-based discussion forums, some web based software and other on-line collaborative tools. Open collaboration is where any user can interact with any other user in a transparent manner. For example, an on-line discussion forum allows a user to post a problem. Another user can read that problem and post an answer. Other users can then build on that answer or provide alternative answers. As a result, users collaborate with each other in a totally open environment to solve problems. Open collaboration is particularly useful for idea management (see below) in large organisations with multiple locations.

Squelching

Squelching is the term for criticising ideas – and it must be avoided at all costs during the idea generation phase. Squelching is telling someone who has just shared an idea with you: "That is a ridiculous idea", "You must be joking" or "They'd never do something like that around here". Squelching is dangerous because it not only demotivates the person who contributed the idea, who will have learned that sharing creative ideas results in criticism, but also other colleagues who will observe the same thing. Clearly a little bit of squelching can do tremendous damage to your innovation strategy.

During the idea generation phase of an ideas campaign or brainstorming session, squelching must be prohibited. Indeed, as much as possible ideas should be praised. Even ideas which are too radical or inappropriate for your organisation should be praised for their creativity.

Only during the evaluation phase (see below) should ideas be open to criticism.

Tools & Techniques

Organisations should have a small "toolbox" of tools and techniques for facilitating innovation. The central tool should be an idea management system capable of soliciting, capturing and evaluating ideas. Properly used, such a tool permits a steady stream of innovative ideas for implementation. Other tools, such as skunkworks, brainstorming, creative spaces and creative meetings further your organisation's innovation potential.

Suggestion Scheme Based Idea Management

Many companies' first foray into the field of idea management is a suggestion scheme based on the old fashioned suggestion box. However, computers have replaced the box. Suggestion schemes are sometimes ad hoc, using a central e-mail address where ideas can be sent for consideration. Other companies invest in building or buying purpose built suggestion scheme software, often boasting so-called web 2.0 functionality.

Unfortunately, such systems are not very effective and tend to fail after 12 to 18 months in my experience. There are several reasons for this.

- There is no structure to idea submission. As a result, the person or team in charge of the system is deluged with suggestions. Because each suggestion has to be analysed individually, the workload on the team is tremendous. Often, the people in charge cannot process the ideas in a timely fashion, giving the impression to idea submitters that the company is not really interested in their ideas.

- Owing also to the lack of structure, a large percentage of ideas are not relevant to current business needs. This results in a high rejection rate.

- There tends to be a high level of repetition. The same ideas are submitted over and over again and they must be repeatedly rejected. If an early submission of the idea is implemented and the submitter rewarded, later submitters feel that they have been cheated of credit for their ideas.

- Factions within the organisation can hijack the system for political, rather than business reasons. This can be done through their submitting large numbers of ideas to support their political agenda, such as launching a project that will give their division resources – even when the project is known not to be viable commercially.

Fortunately, there is an approach to capturing employee ideas that is highly effective. It is based on the well-established principles of creative problem solving (CPS) first devised by Alex Osborn in the 1940s and continually developed by the University at Buffalo.

Campaign Based Idea Management

A superior alternative to the suggestion scheme model of idea management is the campaign based model of idea management. This is based on the well-established principles of Creative Problem Solving (CPS – see Lesson 3). In the campaign based approach, instead of openly soliciting all ideas, the company launches short-term campaigns to solicit ideas on specific issues or problems, for example: "Ideas for new product features that will make our widgets more appealing to young home-owners" or "How can we improve the product documentation in order to reduce customer support demands?"

Campaign based idea management offers two huge benefits over the suggestion scheme approach. Firstly it forces people to think about, and focus their innovation on, strategic business needs. Secondly, it motivates employees to participate by providing specific, time limited challenges. Compare the demands: "Give me an idea" and "Give me an idea on how we can improve our marketing strategy" and it is easy to understand why campaign based idea management attracts more and better ideas.

Your campaign based idea management tool should also provide several other features in order to be effective over the long term.

- **Decentralised management.** Instead of a single innovation manager overseeing all campaigns, it is more effective to empower individual managers to set up and oversee their own ideas campaigns. Firstly, this ensures that the people who will actually implement the ideas are the ones soliciting, capturing and evaluating those ideas. Secondly, it frees the innovation manager from administering campaigns and allows her to focus on the overall innovation strategy of the company.

- **Participation control.** Some challenges should be presented to the entire company which enables your company to tap into the widest range of knowledge, expertise and creativity. Moreover, if yours is a business-to-consumer (B2C) company, your employees are also customers and so see your products and image from multiple perspectives. Other challenges should be open only to particular teams, divisions or locations. Ideas campaigns relating to highly confidential strategic issues should not be open to everyone. Estonian language campaigns about issues affecting the Tallinn office are probably best done in Estonian by employees based there. A properly designed system will enable managers to fine tune ideas campaign participation in this way.

- **Intuitive and easy to use**. Participating in an ideas campaign cannot be made obligatory. Thus, participation must rely on promotion and an easy-to-use tool. If it is not immediately clear how to submit an idea, many people simply will not bother. Idea management software should be easy to use, require as little time as possible for submitting an idea and should not confuse users with unnecessary demands or frivolous features.

- **Semi-anonymous idea submission**. If employees can submit ideas anonymously, they are likely to submit more daring, more creative ideas (see note on creative risk above). Nevertheless, there should be a means of retrieving the name of an idea submitter in the event the idea is implemented. This ensures the appropriate person is rewarded for her creative contribution.

- **Evaluation tool**. In order to determine which ideas should be implemented, the idea management system should have an evaluation tool with the functionality described in the evaluation matrix section below.

- **Flexible idea flow**. It is important to have flexibility in idea flow. Some ideas will clearly have great potential and should be implementable immediately. Others may need a more thorough evaluation procedure to determine feasibility (see Lesson on Idea Quality Control: Evaluation). You idea management system should allow you to act on ideas as needed and not according to a rigid idea flow structure that may not suit your needs.

- **Time Limits.** Ideas campaigns should be limited in duration – usually two to four weeks is sufficient. Time limits motivate people to think about the issue and submit their ideas immediately. Moreover, a steady flow of new ideas campaigns on different issues provides continuous challenges to your most creative thinkers, keeps your idea management programme dynamic and stimulates everyone's imagination.

In addition to focused ideas campaigns, you should also run an on-going open campaign for ideas not relevant to current campaigns. This ensures that random good ideas are captured and implemented.

In order to ensure it is used by as much of the workforce as possible, it is important to promote heavily the idea management system via your communications plan (see above). In addition, managers should promote each individual ideas campaign to ensure employees know about it and are motivated to participate.

Brainstorming

In spite of its continuing popularity, traditional brainstorming is not a particularly effective means to generate creative ideas. Traditional brainstorming can be defined as an event in which a facilitator presents a challenge to a group of people who shout out ideas in a free, unrestricted environment. The facilitator notes down ideas on a whiteboard and the best ideas are selected for implementation.

In tests[1,2] comparing the creative performance of groups of people brainstorming following the traditional method and people writing down ideas individually, the individuals are consistently demonstrated to generate a wider variety of more creative ideas. In other words, if you put eight people in a room together, all writing ideas and other people in a room together all shouting out ideas, the former group (provided all other factors are similar) will always have more creative ideas.

There are several reasons for this: in a large group, there will always be several people who keep quiet or gossip among themselves; a small number of more outgoing people will try to dominate the session; if someone suggests an interesting idea, others tend to ideate around that idea thus restricting the range of creative thinking; and no matter how much you stress the importance of not criticising ideas, members of the brainstorming team will fear that sharing outrageous ideas will subject them to ridicule.

As a result, if you wish to tap into the theoretical advantages of brainstorming, you need to bear in mind the limitations of traditional brainstorming. We have found three effective approaches to group idea generation.

1. **On-line brainstorming** is more effective than traditional brainstorming. Because sharing ideas on-line is more anonymous and similar to writing ideas, on-line brainstorming can in fact be very effective. It also has the advantages of: making it

easy to build upon each others' ideas, unlimited participation and automatic recording of all ideas. Idea management by ideas campaign is an elaboration of this approach.

2. **Non-verbal brainstorming** involves a group of people brainstorming ideas through action rather than words. For instance, brainstormers might build ideas with Lego building bricks or wooden building blocks. They might draw images using a large paper or whiteboard or they might cut out paper to design ideas. We have seen very interesting and enjoyable results with the non-verbal approach.

3. **Individual + collaborative brainstorming** combines private idea generation with group brainstorming. To begin, participants are given a period of time to write ideas on a sheet of paper. Then they are put into pairs to compare ideas and generate more. The pairs are combined into larger groups and the process is repeated. This continues until the entire brainstorming group comes together. Ideas are compared and written on a whiteboard for final comments and additional ideas.

We will look at brainstorming methodology in more detail later in this book.

Creative Spaces

In many organisations, the most creative spaces are the coffee machine zone, the staff canteen and the nearby pub where staff have a drink after work. These spaces provide a relaxed atmosphere for employees to talk about operational inefficiencies, how products and services could be improved and how the working environment could be made nicer. However, these spaces are not designed for productivity. As a result, when staff return to their desks, ideas are soon lost – particularly if there is no idea management tool for capturing ideas.

You should establish in your office(s) creative spaces. They should be comfortable places where people can meet formally or informally to collaborate on ideas, tasks and projects. A creative space can be a corner with a couple of chairs and a small table, a meeting room, a custom built creative room or an outdoor picnic table.

Creative spaces should, at minimum, include whiteboards for making notes, flip-charts for making permanent notes and supplies of paper. At best, they should include coloured paper, scissors, tape, glue, poster paper, post-its, building blocks, toys, modelling clay, music systems and computer terminals. Tools and materials that allow people to throw together quick models are extremely useful for organisations involved in design, engineering or manufacturing.

Not every creative space needs to be completely kitted out. But if at least one creative room is full of tools and materials for creative thinking and construction of ideas, it will provide a useful, productive and creative meeting space.

Skunkworks

A "skunkworks" is a loosely organised corporate research unit or facility that is free to explore any innovative research. Skunkworks aim to innovate and experiment and are not subject to expectations of short term profitability. A skunkworks is typically a place where researchers can experiment with ideas and explore wild possibilities.

Although skunkworks are not consistently profitable, they are highly innovative and periodically develop an idea that is hugely profitable. Some ideas may be too far reaching or outrageous to implement, but they often inspire more practical products and services which are both innovative and immediately marketable.

Many well-known, innovative organisations, such as, Lockheed Martin, IBM, Apple, NASA and HP, to name but a few, have skunkworks.

As an alternative to skunkworks, some companies set aside a small budget for radical ideas. Other companies, most famously Google, allow employees to spend up to a set percentage of their time exploring ideas which have nothing to do with their normal work responsibility. It is from this freedom to explore that many of Google's most innovative ideas have been born.

For an effective innovation strategy, a skunkworks, budget or time allotment for freely exploring innovative ideas is highly recommended. The skunkworks should have a set budget as a percentage of the total budget and should be reviewed on an annual basis to determine how it can be improved.

Skunkworks must be loosely managed and emphasise freedom.

Idea Quality Control: Evaluation

The more successful an idea management system is, the more ideas it will generate. As a result, you need an effective idea quality control system. Some organisations have highly-structured systems comprising multi-stepped procedures for reviewing ideas. While this can be effective, it is also important to retain flexibility in the system. If an idea is clearly a winner, it is often wise to "run with it" immediately, before the competition comes up with the same idea – or learns about yours.

Care should be taken not to over-evaluate ideas. For many organisations, evaluation is about avoiding risk. However, the most innovative ideas with the biggest potential returns on investment inevitably are the most risky. If a highly innovative idea has to go through multiple evaluations and reviews by multiple committees, it is almost certain to be rejected for perceived risk or so heavily modified in attempt to limit risk, that it loses its innovativeness. It goes without saying that it would be a tremendous waste of budget to implement an enterprise innovation strategy only to reject the most innovative ideas that come out of that strategy.

First, Combine Ideas

Before evaluating ideas generated in an ideas campaign, brainstorming event or other activity, the first step should be to combine related ideas that would likely be implemented together. This will most likely be managed by the owner of the ideation activity as she will have the clearest notion of what she wishes to accomplish. Combining ideas simplifies the evaluation process as multiple ideas packaged together as a single large idea can be evaluated as a single entity rather than having to evaluate each component idea individually.

Moreover, combining related ideas often results in a concept that is more than the sum of its parts – and thus offers greater value potential than the individual ideas.

Idea Quality Control Has Several Components.

You are unlikely to make a business case for every idea generated in an idea generation activity. Likewise, a simple evaluation is not going to be sufficient for making a decision that may require considerable investment. Hence, idea quality control typically involves a series of steps or components, each more detailed than the previous.

Quick & Dirty Evaluation

A quick and dirty evaluation is a simple process of comparing ideas to a very basic criterion or set of criteria, such as: "Is this idea a good fit to our business?" or "Can we implement this idea in time for the Christmas shopping period?". Ideas either meet the criteria, and go on to a more formal evaluation, or they do not meet the criteria and are rejected. However, when doing a quick and dirty evaluation, think about every idea you feel does not meet the criteria. Ask yourself whether or not minor changes in the idea might change the situation. If so, modify the idea and pass it on to the next step. If you are not sure whether or not an idea should pass, pass it.

Evaluation Matrix

The 5x5 evaluation matrix is a simple, quick and relatively accurate method for evaluating ideas. You establish five criteria by which an idea can be measured. For example, if evaluating a new product idea, the five criteria might be:

1. How profitable do you expect this new product to be over the next 12 months?
2. How quickly can we get this to market?
3. To what extent does this product represent an advance over our competitors' products?
4. To what extent is this product likely to expand our market share?
5. How good of a fit is this product with our current product line?

In addition, you can give additional weighting to one or more of the criteria.

Ideas are given to a team of expert evaluators. Each evaluator measures how well the idea meets each criterion on a scale of 0 to 5, with 0 being not at all, and 5 being perfectly. This number is the idea's score for the criterion. If a criterion has a higher weighting, multiply the score by that weighting. Add all scores to calculate the idea's total evaluation score. Add the evaluators' combined scores and divide by the number of evaluators to determine the average score.

Evaluators should add additional comments to explain their scores or other issues which should be considered. Evaluations are returned to the person managing the evaluation who compiles all the information into an evaluation report. (In fact, your idea management tool should manage and compile evaluation reports).

If average scores are converted to percentages, then an idea getting 80% or more is typically worth pursuing further. However, other issues also need to be considered. In some cases, an idea might get a relatively low score, but evaluators' comments will offer suggestions which improve the idea sufficiently to make it worth taking further.

For consistency's sake, you should select several evaluation teams, each for evaluating different kinds of ideas (for example, a new product evaluation team, a new marketing concept evaluation team, etc.). This will facilitate comparing ideas and provide a consistent scoring mechanism over the long term.

Some organisations prefer a sequence of three evaluations, with the initial evaluation being a quick overview evaluation and each further evaluation being more detailed. However, care should be taken to avoid over-evaluating ideas as described above.

Open Analysis
If an idea gets a good evaluation score, an open analysis meeting is a good means of determining the next steps and any issues which should be borne in mind during the implementation. The analysis should include the evaluators, the person or people responsible for the idea, the manager who led the campaign and the person who will be in charge of implementing the idea.

The aim of the meeting is to have an open discussion of the idea, potential weaknesses uncovered by the evaluators and to establish a pre-implementation and implementation plan.

Pre-Implementations
Pre-implementations are post-evaluation actions designed to analyse an idea in more depth than is possible with an evaluation. Pre-implementations include:
- Business cases
- Business plans

- Market surveys
- Prototype development and testing
- Trials
- Experiments

Companies normally have pre-implementation procedures in place for testing new products and services. However, they do not always use such procedures for testing operational or other internal ideas. They should. Pre-implementation is an effective means of testing a new idea while minimising the risk.

Existing pre-implementation procedures should be integrated into the innovation machine strategy.

As stated above, sometimes an idea is so clearly revolutionary that it should be implemented immediately. In some cases, this may even mean skipping the pre-implementation phase. Taking an idea directly to implementation is often a means of keeping ahead of the competition. A long, drawn out testing phase allows too many opportunities for your competitors to discover your idea and implement it themselves.

Moreover, when an idea is truly revolutionary – or disruptive (a revolutionary idea which disrupts an entire industry and forces all players to change how they do business. Think of: Amazon for book sales, Dell for PC sales and Skype for Voice over IP (VoIP) telephony), it may not be adaptable to your traditional pre-implementation methods.

Output: Implemented Ideas

Once ideas pass all required quality control processes, they are ready to be implemented. Most companies already have effective implementation procedures for new products, services or operations. If you do not, you should run ideas campaigns on improving these procedures. Interestingly actually implementing ideas is a weakness in many company's innovation strategies.

In addition to implementing good ideas, it is important to...

- Monitor the results of the idea implementations to evaluate the overall innovation programme
- Communicate, via the communication plan, details about new ideas that are being implemented. Be sure to include the names of the people responsible for the ideas, their development and their implementation. Disseminating news about successful implementations of ideas demonstrates the value of the innovation strategy as well as recognises the contributions of the idea submitters.
- Reward people who have submitted and implemented ideas. This can include recognition as well as using any other rewards system you have implemented (see "Establish a rewards scheme" above). Incidentally, you should also reward people who contribute good ideas which you are unable to implement for whatever reasons. This shows that you value their ideas and creative contributions and encourages them to continue to be creative on the organisation's behalf.

Implementation of the Innovation Machine Strategy should result in increased pre-tax earnings of 5%-10% or more if a particularly powerful idea is implemented in a given year. This increased income comes largely from improved operational efficiencies – which are the most frequently implemented ideas in most organisations – and new product ideas. Other ideas may not offer a short term income advantage, but will still benefit the organisation in the short term and, as a result, bring financial advantages over the longer term. For example, ideas which increase employee satisfaction will result in less employee turnover and a more enthusiastic workforce. Ideas which increase the quality of customer service may actually increase costs in the short term, but will bring greater customer satisfaction over the long term, resulting in more sales and fewer returns.

Maintaining the Machine

It is important to monitor the output of your innovation strategy and tweak the strategy over time in order to improve results continually. A major review after six months and annually thereafter allows you to evaluate the results, determine weak points and improve the functioning of your innovation strategy.

For example, if fewer than expected ideas are being captured in ideas campaigns, you will need to look at your communications plan (Do people know about the ideas campaigns?), the usability of your idea management tool (if it is difficult to use, employees won't use it), time (if employees feel they do not have enough time to do their obligatory day to day work, they will not find time to use the idea management tool) and creative risk (Are people afraid to submit ideas?).

Like any machine, the innovation machine needs regular maintenance and tweaking on a regular basis. However, properly maintained, the machine can be expected to function indefinitely.

References
1. M. Diehl, W. Stroebe (1987) "Productivity Loss in Brainstorming Groups: Toward the Solution of a Riddle", **Jouranl of Peronsality and Social Psychology 53, no 3**, pp 497-509

2. M. Diehl, W. Stroebe (1994) "Why Groups Are Less Effective Than Their Members: On Productivity Losses in Idea-Generating Groups", **European Review of Social Psychology 5**, pp 271-303

Phase 3

Motivation

Journey

One Small Step

The chairlift brought Jane and me up to a large wooden platform occupied by a handful of stalls and shops selling food, souvenirs and local handicrafts. A number of people were milling about, looking at the goods and eating.

"Oh my, are they all going to the Temple of Ideas?" asked Jane with some concern.

"No, don't worry," I said. "There are some nice walking trails, a the waterfall – of course – and a Buddhist Temple that all share the mountain with our temple. It's sort of a local tourist site. But those who are not interested in creativity and innovation see the Temple of Ideas as an oddity best left alone."

"That's right," said a smiling, elderly man with a curious accent. "Are you going up to the Temple of Ideas?"

"Yes, we are," said Jane.

"Look up," said the man.

We did. The mountain climbed up into the sky and disappeared in some low-lying clouds.

"You cannot even see your temple, it's so far up!" he continued with a laugh. "And it's a difficult journey. You'll never make it by nightfall. And you don't want to be stuck on the side of the mountain during the night, do you?"

"Uh, no, we don't," said Jane doubtfully, sneaking a quick glance up. "But, surely..."

"Oh don't listen to him!" insisted an elderly woman who joined us unexpectedly. "He's just an old pessimist."

"I am not!"

The two switched to the local language and exchanged some friendly, yet heated words.

The woman continued. "Sure, it's a climb up the mountain. But you two are young and it's early. You'll get up there by dinner time, without a doubt. I am sure of it."

"Ha!" said the man. "You remember, a couple of hikers had to be rescued by helicopter last March. They got stuck halfway up the mountain and spent the night on the trail. One of them was awfully sick afterwards. It gets cold up there at night!"

"But they started late and didn't know what they were doing, you old fool. Anyway, I recognise him," the woman pointed to me. "He's been up and down the mountain many times."

"Well, maybe. But it won't be an easy climb. And for what? A weird temple full of weird foreigners? It's not worth it. Why don't you two stay here and have a drink with me?" The old man gestured towards a café."

"That's what all your fussing is about, isn't it?" Said the woman. "You want them to go to your restaurant."

"Well, it would be easier and more pleasant. No fear of failing to climb the mountain or anything."

"Oh, I don't think they would be very happy that way. You two just ignore my silly husband. He's never gone further than his own restaurant and gets jealous when anyone shows any ambition to conquer the mountain."

"I do not!" he said.

"You do too. Anyway, it's a glorious day and I've heard such nice things about the temple, I'm sure you will have a magnificent climb. And think how wonderful it will feel to look down from the temple and see the clouds below you instead of above you?"

"Indeed!" said I.

Jane smiled for the first time since the conversation with the man had started. "Yes, let's go," she said.

"Well, if you fall off one of the steep footpaths, don't splatter in front of my shop!" said the old man with a mischievous smile.

"Okay," I responded with a smile, while the old woman hit him gently on the arm.

"Just follow that footpath over there," said the woman pointing.

"Thanks," Jane and I said in unison before heading towards the footpath.

Soon we walked round the mountain far enough that the platform and the noise faded as if it had never existed. The view down the mountain was stunning and we could see we were clearly making progress. At the same time, a gap in the clouds allowed us to look right up the mountainside. Suddenly, it did not seem so far away.

"What's the food like in the temple?" Jane asked.

"Stunning," said I. "And after this long hike, it will taste even better still. And there's an impressive wine cellar that is worth the hike alone."

"Marvellous," said Jane speeding up slightly.

Dialogue

Not Enough Ideas

The two company presidents sit opposite each other in a Eurostar train racing across the English countryside. Outside, the scenery zips past in excess of 200 kph. Inside, all is calm and quiet as the two gentlemen sip drinks and chat – in first class, of course.

Alpha: With all this excitement about innovation, I've made one of our junior management types into an innovation manager.

Beta: Good thinking.

Alpha: Thanks, old thing. She's jolly excited too. Already doing this and that in the name of innovation. I might even give her a budget one of these days.

Beta: Probably should. Innovation isn't cheap, you know. But it seems to pay off. For us anyway.

Alpha: Well, I don't know. She managed to download some kind of suggestion software off the web and buy a license awfully cheaply, you know.

Beta: Has she now? Is it any good?

Alpha: Not really. We've had it up and running for a few weeks now. It's hardly collected any ideas – and most of them have been more than a little daft if you ask me.

Beta: Really?

Alpha: Yes, and a number of complaints.

Beta: Oh dear. Have you done anything about it?

Alpha: Well, one idea came from my son you know. He wanted to streamline the invoicing process or something like that. Said it would speed things up payment-wise. I told him not to be so daft. We've been invoicing our clients in the same way for 20 years. They wouldn't like it a bit if we changed things.

Beta: No?

Alpha: I should think not!

Beta: I see.

Alpha: I knew a couple of other people who submitted silly ideas and had a word with them. No point in having an innovation system if we just get daft ideas.

Beta: And, has that improved things?

Alpha: I can't say. Since then we've gone from a trickle of ideas to no ideas.

Beta: Have you considered the possibility that there might be a connection.

Alpha: What do you mean?

Beta: Well, if you are telling people not to be so silly about ideas, it might make them reluctant to suggest more ideas for fear you will just tell them not to be silly again.

Alpha: I don't want silly ideas. I want good ideas. I haven't got time for silly ideas!

Beta: You know, Einstein once said something like "If at first an idea is not absurd, there is no hope for it".

Alpha: Did he now? Well, I suppose he knew a thing or two about ideas.

Beta: One would be inclined to think as much.

Alpha: Actually, old friend. You are making a kind of sense.

Beta: I do from time to time. Just wish my wife would appreciate it.

Alpha: Would you like me to have a word?

Beta: No, I think it's something I've got to deal with myself.

Alpha: Of course.

Beta flags down a train hostess and asks for a couple more drinks.

Alpha: Speaking of having a word, I expect I ought to have one with my son and the others and encourage them to, well, to have more ideas or something.

Beta: I believe it would be in your company's best interests.

Alpha: Easier said than done, though. I suppose your Innovation Mistress...

Beta: Master

Alpha: Sorry, of course. I suppose your Innovation Master has got some ideas on the topic.

Beta: Well, now that you mention it, she has indeed.

Alpha: And I suppose you will tell me to read on in order to glean the relevant knowledge.

Beta: I shall indeed.

Alpha: Okay. Let me find my reading glasses.

Lesson

12 Ways to Motivate for Creativity

Whether you wish people to climb a mountain, have ideas or implement ideas, you need the proper motivation. In the dialogue, Alpha's criticism of his employees' ideas was a powerful demotivator that resulted in fewer ideas and, although he didn't say as much to Beta, it also resulted in a lower level of creativity in ideas. Not surprisingly, if people feel outrageous ideas will be criticised by their superiors, they are less likely to share their ideas than when their bosses embrace originality of thinking.

As an Innovation Master you know all of this of course. You also know that one of your key tasks is to motivate people to participate in all elements of your innovation process. Let us take a look at what you can do to motivate creativity in your company. Here are twelve quick suggestions. A couple of them are explored in more detail elsewhere in this phase.

1. Compliment People Often

Compliment people a lot. By doing so, you present yourself as a positive person who sees the good sides of others. This not only makes you more approachable, but also makes you a more trustworthy person. People know you are unlikely to be critical of their ideas – or them. And that makes them much more willing to share ideas with you.

Arrogant or rude managers, on the other hand, essentially build walls between themselves and the creativity of their subordinates. After all, if your boss is sometimes rude to you, why take a chance sharing a crazy idea with her?

Of course you need to be careful not to be seen as someone who blindly compliments everything. Then you are likely to come across as being out of touch. Compliments must be warranted. But they must also be given generously.

2. Challenge People Often

Most intelligent people thrive on challenges. And creative challenges are particularly.... challenging. If you regularly challenge your subordinates to come up with new ideas, you will exercise their creative minds regularly and make their work environment more interesting.

In particular, in situations where you might once have said, "It cannot be done", ask instead: "How might we do it?" Where once you might have said: "We don't have the budget to do that!" ask instead: "How might we reduce the cost of that idea so that we can fit it in our budget?" or "In what ways might we convince senior management to buy into this idea?"

When preparing a presentation to a client, don't just open PowerPoint on your computer and call up your standard business presentation template. Instead, start by asking your team: "In what ways might we give this presentation real impact?"

When performing routine tasks, ask, "In what ways might we improve this process/make this process more efficient/make this process less time consuming?"

And so on. Constant challenges keep everyone's minds sharp and lead to lots and lots of great ideas on a regular basis.

Importantly, also get in the habit of challenging yourself regularly. It will do wonders for your creative output.

3. Remind People that You Want Ideas

This may seem obvious, but it needs to be done. Always remind people that you are keen to hear their ideas. When you challenge your subordinates, don't stop after the challenge has been issued. Instead follow up with: "I want to hear your ideas", "Let's see how many ideas we can come up with this time!" or similar.

Likewise, in general meetings, always remind people that you are interested in hearing their ideas at any time.

Needless-to-say, when people come to you with their ideas, listen attentively, provide positive feedback and, if there are problems with the idea, challenge the idea owner to solve those problems (see Challenge People Often above)

4. Reward Ideas

Rewarding ideas is an important creativity motivator. Rewards, as you probably know, can range from simple recognition to gifts or special privileges.

You can assign rewards to specific challenges, such as "In what ways might we improve our sales pitch? I have five boxes of chocolates for the five most creative ideas!" Or: "In what ways might we improve product X? Every idea gets an apple!"

Rewards, of course, may also be more structured and associated with idea management processes or structured brainstorming events.

5. Provide Time to Think

A common complaint in many companies launching innovation initiatives is that people claim they do not have time to be creative. Management wants employees to be more creative. Management has invested in idea management tools, innovation training and more for staff. But, employees are so overworked handling day to day tasks, that they do not have time to stop and think. You and I know, however, that thinking is critical for creativity.

Worse, in cubical farms, the employee who is seen staring off into space is likely to be seen as one slacking off rather than one who is hard at work thinking up innovative ideas for the company.

What this all means is that you need to help your subordinates organise and prioritise their time and stress that thinking is a critical component of their job responsibilities.

6. Provide Space to Think and Talk and Create

Tied up with time is space. In 2004, the East of England Development Agency (www.eeda.org.uk) undertook a survey of about 1000 people and found that only 10% had ideas at their desks. Moreover, only 6% of woman and 17% of men had ideas anywhere in the workplace.

Thus you need to provide your subordinates with places where they can think and collaborate on ideas. Such spaces might simply be chairs tucked away in corners or, more elaborately, conference rooms with beanbag chairs and toys in them for people to really relax and think. Better still, where possible, provide picnic tables outside the office and allow people to use them for informal meetings.

7. Go on Creative Thinking Field Trips

Getting out of the office all together is an even better way to inspire new ideas. Employees, at one client of ours, visit spaces where their products are used. There they are challenged to think of new uses for their products, new ways to apply their products and new products that would appeal to their existing clients. This is a great way to generate ideas. Escaping the office brings everyone a breath of fresh air. Visiting environments where your product is used puts you in the mind of your client. And that helps you think in new ways.

You can also visit places not directly related to your business and find inspiration. Art galleries, museums of all kinds and unrelated businesses can inspire ideas. Look at how a restaurant in a small town serves its customers and ask how you might offer the same level of service to your big business customers.

8. Push Ideas

When we are looking for ideas, we have a tendency to stop when we get our first good idea. The problem here is that our first idea is rarely our best or most creative idea.

Hence, when someone comes to you with an idea, ask her to push the idea further or ask "That's a great idea. But you are a creative person. So, think about how else we might accomplish that action and let me know what ideas you generate."

Likewise, if you issue a challenge to your subordinates, ask for another idea for every idea suggested. But, be sure to compliment the suggested idea. The aim is to generate more ideas. Compliments – as we have said already – are great for generating ideas.

9. Implement Ideas

This may seem obvious. But over the years, I have seen a number of organisations and teams go to great length to generate ideas. For example, I've several times seen firms bring together a dozen highly paid managers for a day of brainstorming. The results have been very good with a number of powerful ideas generated.

Over time, however, these companies have managed never even to come close to actually implementing the ideas their managers suggested. In some cases this was due to the perceived risk of the generated ideas. In some cases it was because an easy mechanism for implementing the ideas didn't exist. But most often, it seemed that business-as-usual at these companies had too much momentum and it was simply impossible to change behaviour in order to implement new, unusual ideas.

Not implementing ideas is not only a tremendous waste of resources (think how much it costs to take a dozen managers off their duties for a day), but it is also demotivating in a big way. If subordinates see that ideas are not being implemented, they will quickly learn there is no point in sharing their ideas.

10. Tools

As we have noted before, tools can help employees develop and collaborate on ideas as well as help you capture and manage ideas. Tools can include basic things like whiteboards in meeting rooms for sharing ideas; and pens, markers and paper for working on ideas.

Tools might include mind-mapping software for developing ideas. Medium to large organisations can implement idea management software to capture and manage ideas as well as focus innovation on business needs.

11. Encourage Humour

Creativity and humour go hand-in-hand. Whenever I have led a brainstorming event that has had several teams working on an issue, the team that is laughing the most inevitably has the most ideas. And whenever I participate in a brainstorming event with multiple teams, the team I am working with is usually the team that laughs the most. I am proud of that!

Laughing frees up our inhibitions and makes us feel good. Jokes, like creative ideas, are usually about bringing together dissimilar concepts in new ways. When a group is laughing, participants often try and outdo each other with funny ideas. And those funny ideas are often very creative ideas.

12. Be Creative Yourself – and Demonstrate It!

A good manager leads, of course, by example. If you tell your subordinates to be creative, but never share a creative idea yourself – you are not setting a very good example.

You are certainly a creative thinker. So this last step should not be difficult for you. The question is, are you demonstrating your creativity? Do you bounce ideas off your colleagues – including your subordinates?

If you use creative thinking tools – do you show your subordinates what you are doing and why? If not, it is important that you do. Your subordinates need to see that you are being creative at work. That will make it much easier for them to be creative.

Conclusion

These steps are, for the most part, not particularly demanding. Nevertheless, they can have a powerful effect on your organisation's creativity and innovation. So go ahead and implement a few of them. I expect you will be pleasantly surprised by the results.

Lesson

The Three-Cs

During the monthly sales meeting, Arnold, a new Business Development Executive and something of a gadget freak at Supertrade suggested: "You know those hand-held devices the delivery people at UPS use to confirm receipt of your parcel? Wouldn't it be cool if we had a device like that so we could take clients' orders immediately and send them to the production people? It would make it so much easier to fulfil orders, there would be fewer mistakes and production could begin sooner!"

Steven, a Sales Manager smiled. He was used to outrageous ideas from the sales people. "Do you have any idea how much it would cost to equip the entire sales team with gadgets like that? Not to mention install the infrastructure for taking orders!?"

In less than a minute, Steven has not only rejected Arnold's idea, but has also ridiculed it in public. Steven has sent a very clear message to Arnold and his colleagues: this sales manager is not open to new ideas.

Yet, the scene described is commonplace and almost every creative thinker has experienced it. Many of us, if pushed, will even shamefacedly admit to having been in Steven's place.

Ironically, people like Steven work in companies that describe themselves as innovative, and people like Steven often believe they are supportive of creative thinkers. But a couple of criticisms like the one described and the salespeople will be well trained to keep their creative ideas to themselves. So much for creativity and innovation!

How might Steven have handled the same situation better – and been more receptive to ideas? He could use an approach I call the "Three Cs": Consider, Compliment, Challenge.

First C: Consider
In the example, Steven did not really stop to think about the idea suggested by Arnold. He gave it a quick analysis, found a flaw and rejected the idea.

But analysing is not the same as considering an idea. The latter involves envisioning the implementation of the idea and how it might work. Analysing is more of a score-sheet which gives a pass-fail mark. And if it fails, it fails. Steven should have stopped to think about Arnold's idea, where he felt it was flawed and where it had potential.

Second C: Compliment
Compliments are wonderful things! I try to use them all the time. Compliments make people feel good about themselves and what they are doing. Compliments motivate people to continue to be deserving of the compliment. As a manager, I prefer people to act in the hope of being complimented rather than in fear of being criticised.

Having considered the idea, the manager should compliment it. Ideally, the consideration will generate the compliment. In the case above, "I'm glad you are looking at ways to make the sales process more efficient" would be a good, relevant compliment. But, if nothing else, saying: "That's a good idea." or "It's good you are thinking creatively" are useful standbys.

Third C: Challenge
Having considered an idea and complimented it, the final step is for the manager to challenge the idea suggester to improve the idea. In particular, the manager should look at the issue that triggers criticism.

In the example above, it would be the cost of implementing the idea. Then twist that problem into a creative challenge.

In Steven's case, a far more effective response would be to think for a moment and then say: "Thanks, Arnold. That's a terrific idea and I especially like the fact you are looking at ways to streamline the ordering process. But, the cost of custom making hand-held devices for a relatively small team like ours would probably be way too high. Can you think of ways we might accomplish the same thing but with a reasonable budget?"

In this second scenario, Steven has complimented Arnold in front of his colleagues, has indicated to everyone in the meeting that he is open to ideas and has challenged Arnold to think about his idea in more detail and solve problems that might prevent its implementation.

In a group environment, the Sales Manager might even invite everyone in the room to think about the challenge. And by starting the discussion on a positive note, the manager encourages team members also to take a more positive approach.

Of course, Arnold might find that there is not a viable solution or he may simply not be motivated enough about the idea to take it further. But even if that is the case, he has been motivated to continue being creative. And that is critical for companies that claim to be innovative.

The Three-Cs is a simple, yet remarkably powerful method of establishing an innovation-friendly environment in any organisation. Indeed, I have on several occasions delivered this as a short workshop or a component of a larger training event on several occasions – and the results have always been impressive.

Lesson

When the Best Is Not the Best

Scenario A
Trudy, a manager at Supertrade, needs innovative new product improvement ideas for one the company's cash register models. After thoroughly reviewing customer feedback, competitors' products and a number of other issues, Trudy carefully crafts an excellent innovation challenge. She posts the challenge on her firm's innovation process management web application, inviting all of her colleagues to participate by collaboratively developing ideas on-line. To encourage participation, she also offers several rewards of holidays for two in Paris for the best ideas.

What's wrong with Scenario A? For the most part, it is very good. But, it is likely to produce ideas which are not very creative and which, at best, will result in incremental innovation. To understand why, consider scenario B.

Scenario B
I, Jeffrey Baumgartner, launch a Creative Vegetarian Cooking Competition. I offer several rewards of holidays for two in Paris for the best main course dishes submitted to the competition. I am the only judge.

If you know me or ask my children or friends, you will quickly learn that I am a pasta fiend and, in particular, I often make and thoroughly enjoy spaghetti with a spicy tomato and vegetable sauce flavoured with fresh basil or oregano.

With this information, you get busy in your kitchen, experimenting with various kinds of tomato and vegetable sauce combinations until you come up with something you feel is rather creative. You then submit your dish to the competition.

Most likely, you and most of the participants will have made me a spaghetti with tomato and vegetable sauce or something broadly similar such as linguine with tofu sauce. Submissions may be very good. Indeed, if you've cooked your dish, I am sure it will be absolutely excellent. But as foods go, it probably won't be particularly innovative or creative. But that's not surprising. After all, you followed the instructions to win: make the best dish according to my tastes. So, it is not at all your fault that your dish is not innovative. It is mine.

Now let's consider another similar scenario.

Scenario C

Scenario C is the same as Scenario B, except that instead of offering a reward for the best dish, I offer a reward for the most creative dish; or the most innovative dish.

In Scenario C, you might still want to research my tastes, but you will not be aiming to produce my favourite dinner, you will aim to surprise me with your creative culinary skills. After all that is the stated goal of the competition and you are very creative, as we both know! As a result, your submission for the contest will doubtless be something new, original and delicious!

Best Ideas Are Based on Existing Concepts

The same thing (as Scenario B) happens when employees are told that there will be rewards for the best ideas. They tend to submit ideas that they feel management will like and their judgement is based on their understanding of their managers.

In the case of scenario A, if Trudy is known to be keen on the appearance Supertrade's cash registers, most ideas will focus on the visual appearance of the product. Such changes may well improve upon the existing product, but they are highly unlikely to be breakthrough innovations. That's because colleagues are following Trudy's rules, just as you followed mine in Scenario B.

However, if Trudy wants to have truly innovative ideas submitted to her ideas campaign, she should offer rewards for the most creative ideas or even the most outlandish or crazy or wild ideas. And she must reward accordingly, even if she does not implement the most creative ideas. This, as you can doubtless see, encourages creativity. And it has been confirmed in the laboratory.

Confirmed by Research

In a set of experiments performed in the early 1960s, researchers set up a series of ideation activities and informed one group of participants that they would get higher scores for more imaginative or creative ideas. Participants were further told that their ideas would be scored on two criteria: (1) how unique or different their ideas were and (2) how valuable their ideas were. A control group was given no such instructions and simply brainstormed for ideas. The researchers found that the first group had fewer ideas than the control group; but – more importantly – they had significantly more good ideas.[1]

This is very significant indeed. If Trudy were to change her rewards method in scenario A just slightly, she could expect to get more creaitve ideas with the added benefit of reducing her workload as there would be fewer ideas to evaluate.

It is also an important lesson to bear in mind when launching ideation initiatives in your organisation. Be sure to base rewards on creativity, imaginativeness, uniqueness and/or value added; rather than rewarding for the "best ideas". You'll get fewer, but better ideas!

Reference:
1. V. S. Gerlach, R. E. Schutz, R. L. Baker, G. E. Mazer (1964) "Effects of Variations in Test Directions on Originality Test Response", **Journal of Educational Psychology,** Vol 55 No 2, pp 79-84.

Lesson

Rewarding Innovation

A reward scheme can make or kill an innovation initiative, such as an idea management process. Considering the amount of effort that goes into launching an idea management process in many companies, it is essential to get the rewards right.

In this chapter, we will look at reward schemes supporting an idea management process.

Getting Started with Rewards
In the early days of your idea management initiative, you should reward for quantity rather than quality. Your biggest challenge will be getting your employees to actually log into your idea management system and try it out. If the system is intuitive to use and you launch regular, challenging ideas campaigns (remember: an ideas campaign is an idea management event that begins with a creative challenge, is followed by collaborative idea generation in response to the challenge and concludes with some form of idea evaluation), employees will quickly become regular users. But they need to be lured into the idea management system first.

Thus a small reward such as a little box of chocolates, some fruit or a pen for every idea can be effective. An alternative approach used by an FMCG (fast moving consumer goods) client of my company's was to order a run of special T-shirts they designed to mark their first ideas campaigns with a new idea management system. Everyone who submitted at least one idea got a T-shirt which they were encouraged to wear to work. Indeed, they were even rewarded for doing so. Thus not only did participants receive rewards simply for participating in the initiative, but also they promoted the initiative with their rewards. Such an approach might be enhanced by offering larger rewards to the top idea submitters.

Mid Term Rewards
If such reward schemes will only apply at the early stage of your idea management process, it is important to emphasise this to employees. Otherwise, once you stop complementing ideas campaigns with numerous small rewards, employees may feel you are no longer so interested in their ideas. Nevertheless, you will eventually want to move on to an easier-to-administer rewards scheme.

One such approach is a points-based rewards system in which points are received for submitting ideas. Points might be used like aeroplane frequent flyer miles in that points can be exchanged for gifts, special privileges or the like. A number of idea management software systems include such functionality.

Alternatively, a small gift for each idea submitted, a recognition scheme or rewards for the most active ideas submitters are also effective.

Reward for Creativity
You will probably be tempted at some point to reward the best ideas submitted. This is dangerous and, as we saw in the previous lesson, can actually result in reduced creativity. Don't do it.

A better approach is to offer rewards for the "most creative ideas" or even the "craziest ideas", "most outlandish ideas" or "furthest out of the box ideas". My experience and research both confirm that this approach leads to a higher level of creative thinking and results in ideas that are more creative. That also makes sense: ask for creativity and you get creativity!

Do note, however, that rewarding for creativity may result in a lower number of ideas. When the rewards are for creativity, people are less likely to submit incrementally creative ideas which they know will not be rewarded. This is important to bear in mind if you are looking for incremental improvements rather than creative new ideas.

Big Rewards Are Not Always Good Rewards
In general, offering a substantial cash reward to an individual for a great idea, an implemented idea or anything like that is dangerous. When people know that they can get a massive sum of money for an idea, they tend to act purely for the reward rather than for the company's benefit. When big cash rewards to individuals are on offer, problems such as, managers stealing subordinates' ideas, big disputes between employees and top employees leaving the company out of frustration become commonplace. The result, of course, is poor internal relationships, loss of good staff and collapse of your innovation initiative.

That said, offering teams substantial rewards for developed ideas can be very effective. The reasons why this is the case are clear:

- People are working together as a team to develop a project, thus there is not a rivalry at the individual level for a big pot of money.

- Helping each other develop an idea increases the likelihood of achieving the reward. When an individual gets the reward, the opposite is true.

- When the idea has to be developed into a business plan or other type of project, team members put substantial effort into developing the idea. Hence there is a feeling that the reward is compensation for extra work, rather than a jackpot for one lucky idea instigator.

Transparent Versus Translucent Rewards

Thus far, we have talked about transparent rewards, that is, rewards that are announced at the beginning of any innovation initiative and which are publicly given. If you wish to reward generously a particular individual for her substantial innovative input, translucent rewards are the way to go. A translucent reward might be, as an example, a promotion in which you state, "Sally, we really like the great ideas you have been submitting to the company. As a result, we've decided to promote you to division manager so you can be more hands-on in terms of implementing your innovative ideas."

Such a reward is translucent because it was not advertised across the company and was given privately to Sally. Nevertheless, in giving the reward to Sally, you make it clear that a key reason that she has received the reward of a promotion is her participation in your idea management system.

The most important lesson here is to consider your rewards programme carefully before you launch an ideas campaign or other innovation initiative. A well thought-out rewards scheme will result in a regular flow of creative ideas that could become innovations. A poorly thought-out scheme, on the other hand, can actually work against creativity and innovation and even bring on hard feelings between employees.

Lesson

Good Rewards for the Wrong People

As you doubtless know, rewards are an important element of innovation initiatives. Rewards motivate people to share ideas, develop ideas and implement ideas. When we start new clients up with our idea management software, we stress the importance of rewards in order to encourage idea submission.

Moreover recognition is a particularly important form of reward. Indeed, according to a survey by Robert Half International (1994), "'Limited recognition and praise' was cited as the most common reason for why employees left a company. It was ranked higher than compensation, limited authority, personality conflicts, and all other responses."

So, when you read in the Supertrade company newsletter that Elmer McGillicuty, the vice president for Marketing, has received an Innovation Excellence plaque from the CEO, you might think that the company is motivating people for their contribution to innovation. Sadly, in the case of a large company like Supertrade, you would probably be wrong. In fact, by giving this plaque to Elmer, Supertrade is very likely demotivating people from participating in innovation initiatives.

Who Is Really Doing the Innovation?
That is because in most large companies, high level managers are at best a small part of the innovation process. Actual innovation is being performed by teams of individuals who devise ideas and see them through to implementation. So imagine how employees in Elmer's division feel when they read that he has been given a plaque for innovative work that the employees have performed themselves. After all, the only thing worse than not being recognised for your efforts is seeing someone else being recognised for your efforts! From what I have heard from clients, innovation specialists and even friends, this kind of thing happens a lot. Worse, it is generating a lot of bad feeling which is impeding innovation in many large firms.

The reason that this problem exists is obvious. In companies with thousands of employees, top management does not usually look at the performance of individuals or even teams. Rather they look at the performance of business units or divisions within the company. And when a business unit performs well, they often reward the head of that unit. However, when the organisation is very large, the head of unit is unlikely to have any hands-on participation in innovative projects. Rather she is looking after strategic issues for the unit. This is not to say that the head of unit does not play a part in the innovation process. On the contrary, she plays a very important part. However, it is only a part. And when the many people of the unit see that she is getting all the rewards for their hard work, they are likely to be annoyed. And if the head of unit is perceived (rightly or wrongly) as not really being involved in the innovation process, employees in the unit are likely to be especially annoyed to see her winning rewards they believe they deserve themselves.

Rewards Hierarchy
The solution is not simple. Top management cannot realistically monitor the performance of all individuals and teams in an organisation in

order to identify who is adding what to the firm's innovation initiative. The head of unit, who wins an award, is unlikely to want to give it away to another individual or team in her unit – and in any event, she is probably deserving of an award if she is encouraging innovation in her business unit. However, she is not the sole individual deserving of an innovation award.

The secret of course, is to change the way awards are granted. Vice presidents, heads of units and other people in charge of large numbers of employees should not be awarded for being innovators themselves. Rather they should be rewarded for facilitating innovation. And proof of their merit in facilitating innovation should be based on several factors: the number of innovations coming out of their units, the value of those innovations and, most importantly, the number of people and teams participating in devising, developing and implementing creative ideas that become innovations.

When senior managers are rewarded, as they should be, for helping people to innovate better rather than simply for running innovative divisions, they become motivated to recognise the innovation contribution of their subordinates and to communicate to the company the contributions of those people.

To achieve such results, it is necessary for top management to create a rewards hierarchy that recognises different levels of participation in a company's innovation process. In addition to division heads who facilitate innovation, firms should reward creative thinkers who devise ideas, teams who develop ideas and production people who implement ideas. All of these people contribute to the corporate innovation programme. When they are all recognised and rewarded, they will happily put more effort into innovating.

And that's what you want, is it not?

Phase 4

Ideation

Journey

Bridge Down

Jane and I walked along the winding path through a wood and up the mountain. For much of the time, the trees prevented us from getting a clear view. However, the path eventually led to a stone outcropping devoid of trees. It offered stunning views down the mountainside. We had come a couple of hundred metres higher up the mountain in short time.

"I think I can see the entire town clearly now," said Jane.

"Yes, me too," I agreed. "We've come far in a short while. But we still have some distance to cover. We need to follow the path along the edge there to the spiral staircase at the cliff on the south side. Are you ready?"

"Yes," she said.

"Then let's go."

We followed the trail, for several hundred metres until we came to an area where the footpath had fallen away leaving a gap of about 20 metres or so. All that remained was the rope railing hanging down in the empty space where the path had been.

"Oops!" I shouted. "Watch out. The trail is gone."

We both looked down the face of the mountain and at the remainder of the path across the gap.

"Oh no! How are we going to get across?" asked Jane. It was a good question. The path was gone, the cliff side was sheer and a fall could well be deadly. But it was the wrong question.

"Why do you want to get across?" I asked.

"We need to get to the other side," she answered.

"Why do we need to do that?" I asked.

"Because we need to continue our trek today," she said.

"Why?" I asked.

She paused for a moment. "Because we need to climb up to the Temple of Ideas before nightfall," she said.

"Ah," I said. "That is the true challenge. Now how might we facilitate doing that?"

We both looked around, backtracked on the trail and returned.

"I have an idea," Jane said.

"Good" I said. "Tell me about it."

"The edge of the mountain above us is steep, but it has some footholds. And not far above us, I see another footpath with a wooden railing. I believe we can throw this rope," she pointed at the rope railing hanging over the edge, "over and around one of the wooden posts on the railing above and then tie it down here. Then it should not be difficult to climb up these footholds to the next level."

"Excellent!" I exclaimed. "I think that will work."

It took several throws to get the rope over the wooden post some 10 metres or so above us, but we eventually succeeded. We tied the other end to a metal post that had held the rope railing at our level and it made for a secure loop.

Not wanting to endanger Jane, which would have been bad manners, I started climbing first in order to test the rope and cliff-side. But I need not have been worried about safety. The rope held and the footholds were sufficient to make the climb relatively easy. Moreover, Jane proved a better climber than me. Within a few minutes we were both on the new path. We quickly consulted the map and continued our journey to the Temple of Ideas.

Dialogue

Too Many Ideas

The company presidents are lunching together at a quiet Indian restaurant in London.

Alpha: You know, I followed your advice, or rather your Innovation Master's advice, on motivating people to have ideas.

Beta: I'm glad to hear that. How has it worked out?

Alpha: Got the opposite problem this time.

Beta: Is that so?

Alpha: It is. Otherwise, I wouldn't have said so, old friend.

Anyway, that suggestion software we installed has collected a couple of thousand ideas!

Beta: That's marvellous, isn't it?

Alpha: Not really. They're a real muddle of ideas. Rather confusing, actually. Some ideas are about products, some about operations, some complain about food in the canteen. And, I dare say, a few suggestions were less than complimentary about me!

Beta: You don't say!

Alpha: I do. I just have. Anyway, Diane, the woman I made innovation manager at the firm, tells me that most of the ideas are useless. "Not relevant to business needs," she says. And it's wasting a lot of time going through all the suggestions. Some of our cleverer people, who've been put in charge of reviewing ideas, are complaining that they have got better things to do.

Beta: They probably have.

Alpha: Indeed. A waste of money that software was. Either no ideas or too many useless ones – and we don't dare criticise the useless ones.

I'm beginning to doubt the value of this whole innovation thing. Too much work, not a lot of benefit.

Beta: Oh, don't give up yet. Once you get your innovation process up and running properly, you should get value by the bucket-full. Your problem is not innovation. It's the cheap software.

Alpha: I expect you're right.

Beta: Look at it this way, old thing. Have you ever done any brainstorming?

Alpha: Long ago. These days, everyone gets nervous if I walk into a brainstorming meeting.

Beta: I'm not surprised. You're the president. Anyway, have you ever been to a brainstorming session where the facilitator just demanded ideas, without stating a problem or a challenge?

Alpha: Of course not! That would be ludicrous!

Beta: But that's what your software is doing, isn't it? Just demanding any old idea.

Alpha: Oh, I see. Yes. Quite.

Beta: You'll be wanting software that uses the same principle as brainstorming. My Innovation Master calls the process "Creative Problem Solving".

Alpha: Does she now? And does it work?

Beta: Indeed it does, for us anyway.

Alpha: And how does it work?

Beta: Just read the next chapter.

Alpha: Somehow, I thought you'd say that.

Lesson

Creative Problem Solving

As we saw in Alpha and Beta's dialogue, when managers decide to capture employee ideas, they often start by setting up an electronic suggestion box which invites anyone to submit any idea whatsoever. As Alpha observed, this often results either in very few ideas or a great many ideas, most of which are less than relevant to business needs.

Creative ideas do not suddenly appear in people's minds for no apparent reason. Rather, they are the result of trying to solve a specific problem or to achieve a particular goal, such as Jane's working out how to deal with the collapsed footpath. She had to accomplish several quick tasks. Firstly, she needed to identify the correct problem – which was not the same as her immediate assumption. Then she had to generate ideas and finally she had to evaluate them to identify the idea that would best solve her particular problem. Because Jane is a natural creative thinker, she was able to do much of this in her head.

In fact, this process is called "Creative Problem Solving (CPS). Not only can (and should) individuals use it to solve personal problems, but also teams, groups and even entire companies can use it to facilitate the front end of their innovation process.

CPS is a simple process that involves breaking down a problem to understand it, generating ideas to solve the problem and evaluating those ideas to find the most effective solutions. Highly creative people like Jane tend to follow this process in their heads, without thinking about it. Less naturally creative people simply have to learn to use this very simple process.

Although creative problem solving has been around as long as humans have been thinking creatively and solving problems, it was first formalised as a process by Alex Osborn, who invented traditional brainstorming, and Sidney Parnes. Their Creative Problem Solving Process (CPSP) has been taught at the International Center for Studies in Creativity at Buffalo College in Buffalo, New York since the 1950s.

CPS Steps

However, there are numerous different approaches to CPS. Mine is more focused on innovation (that is the implementation of the most promising ideas) than pure creativity. It involves seven straightforward steps.

1. Clarify and identify the problem
2. Research the problem
3. Formulate creative challenges
4. Identify insights
5. Generate ideas
6. Combine and evaluate the ideas
7. Draw up an action plan
8. Do it! (ie. implement the ideas)

Let us look at each step more carefully.

1. Clarify and identify the problem

Arguably the single most important step of CPS is to identify your real problem or goal. This may seem easy, but very often, what we believe to be the problem is not the real problem or goal. For instance, a sales manager at Supertrade may feel that people in her department are not making enough sales. But in order to solve the problem, she needs to know why this is the case. Are they not getting sufficient leads? Are existing customers not returning owing to dissatisfaction? Has a competitor come up with a breakthrough innovation that leaves Supertrade's products looking poor in comparison? Or is it something else? Different problems demand different solutions.

Five Whys

The first thing to do with any problem is ask "Why is this a problem?" five times. This will enable us to identify the negative consequences of the problem. The Sales Director at Supertrade might ask "Why is it a problem that we are not selling enough of our products?"

1. Sales revenues are below operational costs.

That is definitely a problem! But, we need to ask this question five times. So let's ask "Why else?"

2. We cannot finance the growth of our company.
3. We are losing market share to the competition
4. Our sales people are becoming demotivated, making it even harder for them to sell.
5. We are in danger of losing our existing customers to the competition.

Now we have a clear view of the consequences of insufficient sales. Clearly the most worrying is the first why: insufficient income. But all of these are relevant and indicate a clear need to generate more income.

Why Has This Occurred? x 5

We now need to try and understand why the problem has occurred. So, we ask the question, "Why has this occurred?" five times. This ensures that we think about the problem in detail. Very often the first reason we give for a problem is not the primary reason. By digging deeper, we can get to the root causes of a problem and devise a creative challenge that addresses them.

So, we ask the management team at Supertrade, "Why has it occurred that you are not selling enough of your products?" The initial reaction might be to blame the sales people:

1. Sales people are not performing well enough.

But if we dig deeper and, ideally include a sales person on the problem deconstruction team, we are likely to learn more about the causes of Supertrade's poor sales. They respond:

2. Ever since we cut back on our marketing budget, we've been getting far fewer leads.
3. Sales people are not generating enough good leads to get sales
4. New sales people are not getting any training at Supertrade.
5. Clients are cutting their budgets.

How Urgent Is the Problem?
We need to determine the urgency of the problem. This is unlikely to affect the challenge itself, but it can speed up the innovation process and is highly valuable during the evaluation phase of the process. If the problem is urgent, solutions need to be quickly implementable. In this case, it would seem the problem is indeed urgent.

What Are Your Competitors Doing About This Problem?
It's always a good idea to see how your competitors are dealing with the situation. Do they seem also to be having trouble selling? This information can be difficult to glean. But by listening to clients, watching

for tell-tale signs (such as deep discounting and laying off staff) you can often get an idea of your competitors' situations.

In any event, you probably do not want to take the same action against the problem as one or more of your competitors has done. Leaders do not become leaders by following other firms. They lead! And innovators do not copy their competitors. They are copied by their competitors!

Of course if your competitors appear to be suffering the same problem you are – such as during an economic downturn – your swift, innovative solution is likely to maintain your leadership in the market or propel you to leadership if your firm is not already there. That leaves your competitors to follow in your footsteps or find an alternative innovative solution.

In our example, we'll assume Supertrade's competitors are also seeing reduced sales and suffering for it.

Putting It All Together

At this stage, we have quite a lot of information. We have a problem, a list of consequences resulting from the problem, a list of reasons the problem has occurred, a sense of urgency and the knowledge that our competitors are similarly suffering, indicating that there is a real opportunity to take the innovative lead in this situation.

Criteria

At this stage, you should have a clear notion of what the real problems are. Now you should decide what criteria you will eventually use to evaluate or judge the ideas. Are there budget limitations, timeframe or other restrictions that will affect whether or not you can go ahead with an idea? What will you want to have accomplished with the ideas? What do you wish to avoid when you implement these ideas? Think about it and make a list of three to five evaluation criteria. Then put the list aside. You will not need it for a while.

2. Research the Problem

The next step in CPS is to research the problem in order to get a better understanding of it. Depending on the nature of the problem, you may need to do a great deal of research or very little. The best place to start these days is with your favourite search engine. But do not neglect good old-fashioned sources of information and opinion. Libraries are fantastic for in-depth information that is easier to read than computer screens. Colleagues, associates, friends and family can also provide thoughts on many issues and the non-colleagues often provide a fresh perspective on the problem. Forums on sites like LinkedIn and elsewhere are ideal for asking questions. There's nothing an expert enjoys more than imparting her knowledge. Take advantage of that. But always try to get feedback from several people to ensure you get rounded information.

3. Formulate One or More Creative Challenges

At this stage, we have quite a lot of information. We have a problem, a list of consequences resulting from the problem, a list of reasons the problem has occurred, a sense of urgency and the knowledge that our competitors are similarly suffering, indicating that there is a real opportunity to take the innovative lead in this situation. We have also collected a lot of additional information through our research. Now it is time to put everything together and formulate some creative challenges. This is arguably the single most important step of CPS. A well formulated challenge that deals with a clearly identified problem virtually guarantees you will get relevant ideas when it comes time to generate ideas.

The key issues in Supertrade's sample problem are clear:

1. The company needs to generate more income. This would normally be done by selling more units of the product in question.
2. Sales people are not getting the leads they need to generate sales, nor are new ones being sufficiently trained to generate those leads themselves
3. Customers have lower budgets and so are unable to spend as much on Supertrade's products as you would like.

Each factor represents an underlying problem and so deserves a challenge of its own. The first factor is that the firm needs to generate more income. Although this normally comes through sales of the product, there may be other ways of generating income. Hence we can formulate a challenge like this:

1. In what new ways (ie. other than selling our products) might we generate income?

The second factor actually includes two problems: the sales people are not generating leads and new people are not being sufficiently trained. The latter problem does not require creativity to solve. Supertrade can provide them with more training. Nevertheless, we would hope the training itself will be creative! However, the first problem clearly suggests a challenge.

2. How might the sales people generate more leads?

The third factor would at first seem to be the customers' problems. They do not have enough money to buy Supertrade's products. But with a little thought, this problem actually suggests a wonderful challenge for Supertrade:

3. In what ways might we make it financially easier for our customers to buy our products?

Each of these challenges deserves a separate ideation event – such as an ideas campaign, brainstorm or other activity – assigned to it. However, the order in which you tackle each challenge is important. Challenge 1 should certainly go first. Alternative income generation models may include leasing your products rather than selling them or offering products as a part of a service package or not making products at all and rather licensing the right to make the products to others.

Next, Supertrade should tackle challenge 3 and identify ways to make it easier for customers to buy their products. Very likely this ideas campaign will generate similar ideas to the first! That's not surprising. Both challenges are addressing a very similar issue, but from different perspectives.

Once ideas from these two campaigns have been clustered and evaluated in order to identify those ideas that offer the most value, it is time to tackle challenge 2: how to generate more leads. This challenge is last because the innovations in income generation will affect they way the product is sold and, indeed, may suggest some suitable lead generation approaches. For instance if Supertrade decides to sell their product as a service in exchange for a low monthly fee, sales people can use this information in their lead generation methods.

The Challenge of Challenges

This last step of transforming the key factors into challenges is something of an art form and it takes practice. There are no clear cut rules. However, potential challenges should meet a few key criteria.

- A challenge should be a short, concise question.

- A challenge typically begins with "In what ways might we..?" or "How might we...?" or "What new...might we...?"
- A challenge addresses only a single issue. If there are two issues involved, the challenge should be split into two separate ones.
- A challenge should neither be so broad as to invite irrelevant solutions nor be so narrow as to prevent any potential solutions from fitting it.
- A challenge should not include the evaluation criteria you prepared. These should be saved for the evaluation process itself.

As you become accustomed to deconstructing problems into challenges, you will find it becomes more and more natural. And once this happens, the process becomes easier and that, in turn, makes it easier for you and your colleagues to innovate on behalf of your firm.

4. Identify Insights and Inspiration

You are almost ready to start generating ideas, but before you work on ideas in response to your challenge, think about what might provide insight and inspiration that will help you generate ideas. Some forms of inspiration are unrelated to the challenge. For instance, I like to go for long walks for inspiration. I also find the music of Bach provides me with deeper vision into problems. Other people like to lie down or take a bath. Whatever works for you is great.

You may seek inspiration before you generate ideas, for instance by reading up on research related to the problem. Or you might seek inspiration during the idea generation session by brainstorming in a beautiful location. If the challenge is a B2B (business-to-business) issue, why not brainstorm in one of your customers' premises?

5. Generate Ideas

Finally, we come to the part most people associate with brainstorming and creative problem solving: idea generation. In the corporate environment, we usually associate idea generation with brainstorming. But there are several approaches to idea generation in CPS. In other lessons, we will take a peek at the basics of brainstorming, visual brainstorming and ideas campaigns.

However, you can also generate ideas solo. It is worth understanding how this works as it should be an element of group idea generation as well. For instance, traditional brainstorming is typically more effective if you allow each participant time to generate ideas on her own, prior to the idea shouting match.

Generating Ideas Solo

Take only one creative challenge. Give yourself some quiet time and try to generate at least 50 ideas that may or may not solve the challenge. You can simply write them down in linear fashion, write them down on a mind-map, enter them onto a computer document (such as MS Word or OpenOffice) or use specialised software for idea generation. The method you use is not so important. What is important is that you follow these rules:

Write Them Down

Write down every idea that comes to mind. Even if the idea is ludicrous, stupid or fails to solve the challenge, write it down. Most people are their own worst critics and by squelching their own ideas, make themselves less creative. So write everything down. **No exceptions!**

No Squelching

If other people are also involved, insure that no one criticises anyone else's ideas in any way. This is called squelching, because even the tiniest amount of criticism can discourage everyone in the group for sharing their more creative ideas. Even a sigh or the rolling of eyes can be critical. Squelching must be avoided!

Be careful not to squelch – or criticise – yourself. You are probably your own worst critic and may well decide not to write down some ideas because you feel they are too weird, irrelevant or simply not suitable. Do not allow this to happen.

If you are working alone, don't stop until you've reached your target of 50 (or more) ideas. If you are working with other people, set a time limit like 15 or 20 minutes. Once you have reached this time limit, compare ideas and make a grand list that includes them all. Then ask everyone if the have some new ideas. Most likely people will be inspired by others' ideas and add more to the list.

If you find you are not generating sufficient ideas, give yourself some inspiration. A classic trick is to open a book or dictionary and pick out a random word. Then generate ideas that somehow incorporate this word. You might also ask yourself what other people whom you know, such as your competitor, your sweetheart, a friend or a character on you favourite TV show, might suggest.

Idea generation does not need to occur at your desk. Take a trip somewhere for new inspiration. Find a nice place in a beautiful park. Sit down in a coffee shop on a crowded street corner. You can even walk and generate ideas.

In addition, if you browse the web for brainstorming and idea generation, you will find lots of creative ideas on how to generate creative ideas!

One last note: if you are not in a hurry, wait until the next day and then try to generate another 25 ideas, preferably in the morning. Research has shown that our minds work on creative challenges while we sleep. Your initial idea generation session has been good exercise and has certainly generated some great ideas. But it will probably also inspire your unconscious mind to generate some ideas while you sleep. Don't lose them!

6. Combine and Evaluate Ideas

After you have written down all of your ideas, take a break. It might just be an hour. It might be a day or more. Then go through the ideas. Related ideas can be combined together to form big ideas (or idea clusters).

Then, using the criteria you devised earlier, choose all of the ideas that broadly meet those criteria. This is important. If you focus only on the "best" ideas or your favourite ideas, the chances are you will choose the less creative ones! Nevertheless, feel free to include your favourite ideas in the initial list of ideas.

Now get out that list of criteria you made earlier and go through each idea more carefully. Consider how well it meets each criterion and give it a rating of 0-5 points, with five indicating a perfect match. If an idea falls short of a criterion, think about why this is so. Is there a way that it can be improved in order to increase its score? If so, make a note. Once you are finished, all of the ideas will have an evaluation score. Those ideas with the highest score best meet your criteria. They may not be your best ideas or your favourite ideas, but they are most likely to best solve your problem or enable you to achieve your goal.

Depending on the nature of the challenge and the winning ideas, you may be ready to jump right in and implement your ideas. In other cases, ideas may need to be developed further. With complex ideas, a simple evaluation may not be enough. You may need to do a SWOT (strengths, weaknesses, opportunities and threats) or discuss the idea with others who will be affected by it. If the idea is business related, you may need to do a business case, market research, build a prototype or a combination of all of these.

Also, bear in mind that you do not need to limit yourself to one winning idea. Often you can implement several ideas in order to solve your challenge.

7. Draw Up an Action Plan

At this point, you have got some great ideas. However, a lot of people have trouble motivating themselves to take the next step. Creative ideas may mean big changes or taking risks. Some of us love change and risk. Others are scared by it. Draw up an action plan with the simple steps you need to take in order to implement your ideas. Ideas which involve a lot work to implement can be particularly intimidating. Breaking their implementation down into a series of readily accomplished tasks makes these ideas easier to cope with and implement.

8. Do It!

This is the simplest step of all. Take your action plan and implement your idea. And if the situation veers away from your action plan steps, don't worry. Rewrite your action plan!

Lesson

Brainstorming

Brainstorming is the traditional way to generate lots of ideas on a specific issue and then determine which idea – or ideas – is the best solution. Brainstorming is most effective with diverse groups of 8-12 people and should be performed in a relaxed environment. If participants feel free to relax and joke around, they'll stretch their minds further and therefore produce more creative ideas.

A brainstorming session requires a facilitator, a brainstorming space and something on which to write ideas, such as a white-board, a flip-chart or software tool. The facilitator's responsibilities include guiding the session, encouraging participation and writing ideas down.

Brainstorming works best with a diverse group of people. Participants should come from various departments across the organisation and have different backgrounds. Even in specialist areas, outsiders can bring fresh ideas that can inspire the experts.

Assuming you have followed CPS (see previous Lesson), you will have a well-defined creative challenge ready and waiting for ideas. You should announce the challenge to the participants in advance so they have time to think and research the issue.

Creativity exercises, relaxation exercises or other fun activities before the session can help participants relax their minds so that they will be more creative during the brainstorming session.

Traditional Approach

In a traditional brainstorming session, the facilitator writes the challenge on a whiteboard and then invites all participants to shout out solutions while the facilitator writes them down on the whiteboard. There must be absolutely no criticizing of ideas. No matter how daft, how impossible or how silly an idea is, it must be written down. Laughing is to be encouraged. Criticism is not.

Typically, the aim should be to generate as many ideas as possible within a set time frame, such as 30 minutes. Alternatively, you can set a target number of ideas, such as 100.

The Problem with the Traditional Approach

The traditional approach to brainstorming has been around since the 1950s and is still used frequently today. However, there is a slight problem with this approach. It has been proven again and again not to work!

- **Poor facilitation.** Even trained facilitators who do not understand creative problem solving (CPS) are often unable to manage properly a brainstorming event.
- **Waiting.** When one person shouts out an idea and the facilitator writes it down, other participants have to stop and listen before sharing their own ideas. At best this slows things down. At worst, people forget their ideas while waiting or are afraid to share their ideas which they feel are overly different to the idea they just listened to.
- **Squelching.** Criticising ideas during the idea generation phase of brainstorming demotivates everyone. It tells participants that wacky ideas will get you in trouble. The thing is: the wackiest ideas are the most creative. So, any squelching basically communicates to participants that creative ideas are not

wanted. And participants oblige by suggesting uninspiring and predictable ideas.

- **Dominating personalities.** If one person dominates the brainstorming session, her ideas inevitably become the focus and other participants' ideas are pushed to the side. Unfortunately, this means that only one person is really doing any brainstorming - and that makes nonsense of bringing a brainstorming group together. Worse, dominating people are usually more interested in power than in discovering the best ideas.

- **Topic fixation.** When someone suggests an obviously good idea in a brainstorming event, other people tend to focus on similar ideas. The result is that other avenues of possibility are ignored.

- **Too much noise.** In a good brainstorming event, a lot of people are sharing ideas loudly. That means everyone has to listen to other ideas before sharing their own. The result is more time and energy is spent on listening and interpreting ideas than on generating ideas. Worse, quiet or shy people tend to keep to themselves when brainstorming gets noisy - so you lose their ideas.

My Approach

My approach, which avoids these problems, is to have participants spend 10 to 15 minutes generating ideas on their own. Then put them in pairs, have them compare ideas and add any more that come to mind. Then combine the pairs into bigger groups in order, again, to share ideas and add more. Continue in this way until you have one group that comprises the entire brainstorming team. At this time, put all existing ideas on the whiteboard. Combine similar ideas and avoid repeating ideas. Then finish off with a 15-20 minute traditional brainstorming shouting match to catch any ideas inspired by the collection.

Throughout this process, ensure that there is no criticism and no squelching. As facilitator, be sure to compliment every idea equally.

Other Approaches

There are a variety of other approaches to brainstorming, such as the Post-it method. Here, participants write ideas on Post-its and stick them to a wall. Then the facilitator leads a discussion in which similar ideas are combined. This is typically followed by a second round of idea submission, where participants are inspired by ideas from the first round. This avoids some of the flaws with traditional brainstorming. However, it also sometimes lacks the energy and collaboration of traditional brainstorming as people are generally working alone.

Other facilitators have created variations on these approaches. Inevitably, such approaches follow CPS methodology.

Brainstorm No-Nos

There are a handful of issues to avoid in a brainstorming session.

- **Bosses.** No matter how cool you are as a boss, you almost certainly intimidate your subordinates on some level. As a result, if you sit in on a brainstorming session, your subordinates are likely to restrain themselves for fear of sounding foolish. If you absolutely must participate, be sure to emphasise that the company is at this time specifically looking for outrageous ideas – the wackier the better and then do not even hint at criticising anything!

- **Interruptions.** Ensure that mobile telephones are switched off and that office assistants understand that the brainstorming meeting is not to be disturbed for anything less than nuclear war. Actually, situating the event outside the office and confiscating communications devices beforehand can be an excellent approach.

- **Squelching.** We've covered this already, but I cannot stress enough that squelching can destroy an idea generation session. If you are facilitating a brainstorm, you must be willing to stamp down on squelching, even if it is coming from a superior (as it often is!).

For the best results in a brainstorming session, invest in a professional facilitator. Her fees will probably be less than the costs of staff time invested in the activity and, if she is good, will show an impressive return in terms of idea quality. However, before you come to an agreement, ask her how she overcomes the brainstorming problems we've covered here.

If you really must do your own brainstorm facilitation, at least practice on a trail group or two before running a real event. This will help you hone your technique and build confidence.

Conclusion

Brainstorming can be an effective and enjoyable means of generating creative ideas through collaboration. However, it is important to bear in mind the inherent weaknesses of traditional brainstorming techniques and find an approach that overcomes these problems.

Lesson

Visual Brainstorming

As we learned in the previous lesson, traditional brainstorming is not usually very effective. One way to avoid the pitfalls of this approach is to do away with the words all together and focus on brainstorming involving non-verbal idea generation. That is, rather than expressing ideas in words, participants express ideas in images, models or actions. You might use objects which teams put together to solve problems. You might use arts and crafts materials such as coloured construction paper, tape, string, card, pens and the like. You might use people to create improvisational role plays.

An Example

Let's imagine that Supertrade wants to brainstorm ideas for unmanned checkout scanning devices (in other words, a device that would allow customers to get their products scanned and pay by credit/debit card without using a sales clerk. Rather than running a brainstorming session where people shout out ideas or write ideas on post-it's and stick them to the wall, you set up a visual brainstorming activity.

The first step, of course, is to frame the creative challenge, for example: "What might our unmanned checkout device look like?" This done, you bring together a diverse group of a dozen people from various divisions in the company as well as a few typical customers. You provide them with a huge pile of Lego building bricks and have them work together to build a model of the device brimming with new feature ideas. Instead of shouting out ideas, the team works together to build the checkout device with Lego bricks. As with verbal brainstorming, each member should be encouraged to participate and try out new ideas. Likewise, criticism must be forbidden. Talking, on the other hand, is perfectly acceptable. But, bear in mind that ideas must be implemented in the Lego model and not simply vocalised.

The checkout device that the team builds will probably look nothing like the company's existing ones. But it will probably be bursting with ideas. (Note: actually, in the author's experience, the team will probably break off into sub-teams each building their own models - but that's okay. Indeed, if the initial team is large the facilitator should separate it into multiple diverse teams anyway).

Once the model is completed, speaking is allowed. The team presents its ideas, explains the features and, where relevant, the logic behind those features. Finally, all of the ideas together with images of the Lego models are compiled into a report -- unless the company's management is open minded enough to accept a Lego model in lieu of a report!

The advantages to visual brainstorming in the example given include:

- There are fewer distractions. No one needs to wait for someone else to speak. Everyone can focus on building.

- No one can sit quietly in the background. Unlike in a verbal brainstorming event where quiet people hide behind the noise, in a visual brainstorming event, it is obvious who is participating and who is not.

- It is harder for anyone to dominate when everyone is building bits and pieces. People who attempt to dominate vocally will be unable to keep pace with the visual development of the ideas and so, will actually, provide less involvement with the end result.

- In the author's experience, there is far less squelching in visual brainstorming. Probably this is because visual brainstorming is fun, requires a high level of personal concentration and people find it harder to criticise visual ideas than verbal ideas.

Various Approaches

Visual brainstorming need not be limited to physical objects such as new products. You may also use it to brainstorm processes, services and activities. All you need is a little imagination and the ability to visualise problems. Here are a few examples.

- **Supertrade wants to design a complete checkout station, with cash register, scanner and clerk, that speeds up the payment process in supermarkets.** The team can be provided with dolls, building blocks, paper and other supplies. They can then use the building blocks to simulate the checkout stations and the dolls to demonstrate the flow of people through the checkout.

- **Supertrade wants to improve internal communications, particularly across international offices.** Lego can be used to create representations of divisions, communications methods and the strength of communications. Alternatively, construction paper, tape and small crafts tools can be used to build representations of divisions and string can be used to show the path of communications. As with the above example, the brainstormers can modify the existing model to improve it - or start from scratch and build a better system.

Clearly, there is substantial room for creative thinking in the approach you take to visually brainstorming a problem. And it is worth investing your time in devising a good approach. After all, a creative brainstorming approach is likely to motivate participants to be extra creative in their ideas.

The tools you use in a visual brainstorming event might include any or all of these:

- Children's construction toys such as building blocks, Lego, etc.
- Dolls and action figures to represent people.
- String, wire, yarn to represent connections.
- Satay sticks to represent directions.
- Construction paper.
- Tape.
- Modeling clay.
- Cups.
- Bits of fabric, buttons and other sewing materials.
- Pipe cleaners.
- Wire mesh.
- Boxes of various sizes.
- Toy cars.
- And anything else you can get your hands on.

Children's toys, in particular, can be useful as well as encourage creative thinking. Indeed, you would do well to spend some time in a toy shop when planning your visual brainstorming activity.

Role Play

Once one or more concepts have been developed through visual brainstorming, you can develop ideas further through role play. For instance, once the Supertrade brainstormers come up with some ideas for unmanned checkout stations, they could then build a full size simulation – it does not need to be fully functional so even a cardboard model would suffice. Then the brainstorm team would play the role of shoppers using the new system.

This will better enable them to see the new ideas from the end users' perspective and will very likely inspire additional creative thinking that can be applied to the end concept.

Conclusion

Visual brainstorming can be an effective approach to idea generation. In my experience, it is more fun, people become more involved and more thought is spent focusing on the challenge. Interestingly, I have also noticed that when visual brainstormers present their ideas, they often do so in the form of a story describing their models. Traditional brainstormers, on the other hand, tend to announce a list of ideas.

That said, visual brainstorming requires a higher level of creativity in the planning stage in terms of devising an effective approach and appropriate tools. Moreover, socially conservative business people may be reluctant to play with children's toys and may need to be convinced of the value of the activity.

Visual brainstorming also requires a certain level of confidence from the facilitator and an ability to keep things under control, encourage participation and answer questions from participants who have never done anything like this before. Your best approach would be to run some trail visual brainstorming events with friends, sympathetic colleagues, students or other groups who can provide useful feedback.

Lesson

Ideas Campaigns

When Supertrade or the large companies run by Alpha and Beta want to involve large groups of people in various locations in idea generation, brainstorming is no longer practical. Ideas campaigns, on the other hand, can be very effective. Ideas campaigns are structured events designed following creative problem solving (CPS) methodology combined with business analytics. The result is an effective approach for generating ideas in a collaborative space and then evaluating them in order to identify and combine the ideas with the greatest profit potential.

In most cases, an ideas campaign is delivered by idea management software that allows you to run regular ideas campaigns as an integral part of your ongoing innovation process.

This is how an ideas campaign works in a nutshell:

1. Preparation
As with any approach using CPS, the first part of an ideas campaign is to clarify your actual problem and formulate it in a challenge.

2. Promotion
Once the challenge has been formulated, you need to promote it to participants. This can be done via email, internal announcements and similar. Small rewards for participation can be announced in order to encourage participation. It should be noted that a typical problem with an ideas campaign is a low level of participation. In part, this is be-

cause managers expect everyone to submit ideas. In fact, 30% participation is very good.

Promotion is a key issue with your entire innovation process and not just ideas campaigns. Please refer to "Motivating People to Participate" in the Lesson on "Drafting an Innovation Plan" for more details.

3. Collaborative Idea Sharing

This is where ideas are submitted. But rather than shouting them out, participants enter ideas into on-line forms. Usually, people can also collaborate on colleagues' ideas by adding comments or "building blocks" to specific ideas. This allows cross-enterprise collaboration and can really spark some interesting ideas.

Some idea management tools even allow people to develop ideas in a Wiki-like environment. In other words, rather than adding a separate building block to an existing idea, a collaborator can edit the existing idea directly, adding her thoughts and building idea as a collaborative document.

4. Evaluation

Good idea management software using the ideas campaign approach will include tools for evaluating ideas according to your criteria (see first lesson on Innovation Plan). If not, ideas will have to be exported and ranked according to how well each meets your business needs.

Conclusion

An ideas campaign is a single event that typically lasts from two to four weeks and follows CPS methodology. The advantage is that large numbers of people can participate and well-designed idea management software will streamline the process, making the management of so many ideas relatively easy.

Lesson

KISS:
Keep Ideas Simple, Sweetheart

One of the underlying maxims of engineering is that of KISS, an acronym for "Keep It Simple, Stupid" or, as I prefer: "Keep It Simple, Sweetheart". And if you have ever watched a project evolve from concept to design to implementation, you will understand the importance of KISS. When new ideas are at the drawing board, they are often simple, elegant concepts. But, as more people become involved, they all want to add features to the concept. As a result, the design must become increasingly complex in order to support all the proposed features.

However, many of those proposed features will prove useless. They will add complexity to the design of the project, they will make the finished product more expensive to purchase and maintain and they will offer no real benefits to the end user.

Chocolate Cake

For example, let us imagine your team wants to make a chocolate cake. You begin to compile the recipe with ingredients such as: flour, sugar, eggs, baker's chocolate and the like. Suddenly, a team member says: "Let's add walnuts. Chocolate cake with walnuts is yummy!"

And another team member suggests: "Why don't we give it a whipped cream centre? I had a chocolate cake last week with a whipped cream centre and it was probably the best chocolate cake I've ever had."

Meanwhile others suggest peanut-butter frosting, adding coconut flakes, layers of strawberry jam, shredded carrots on the top, making the cake in the shape of a heart, roasting the cake over an open fire, and so on.

Before you know it, the simple chocolate cake you began making is turning into a culinary disaster which will require a supermarket full of ingredients, take all day to make and will almost certainly taste terrible.

One way or another, the group needs to keep their cake simple and that will mean reducing the number of suggested ingredients and devising a simple, but tasty chocolate cake – probably focusing on quality ingredients and careful preparation rather than an excess of ingredients and convoluted preparation.

Too Many New Features

This is a lesson we should bear in mind when innovating. When looking at how to improve products or services we are almost inevitably looking for ways to make those products more complex. I have been using word processors for more than 20 years, including around a dozen years of Microsoft Word. In all that time, I have never seen a company roll out a simpler word processor – even though the number of new features introduced over the past ten years has been minuscule, offering no real added value, particularly in view of their added complexity. Indeed, my heart goes out to people – such as my neighbour – only now learning how to use MS Word. The number of absolutely useless features they face will only reinforce their beliefs that computers are overly complex.

KISS!

In fact, when next brainstorming new product and service features, don't ask "What new features can we add to product X?" or "What new services can we offer to our customers?" Rather, ask "How can we make our product simpler to use?" or "How can we make our range of services simpler for our clients to understand."

And it goes without saying that you should always be asking "How can we make our operations simpler?", "How can we make our supply chain simpler?"

Indeed, simpler products and services not only benefit your clients, who often find simpler goods easier to use effectively, but also benefit you. If you can simplify product X so it requires fewer parts, you reduce your manufacturing costs. If your customers can understand your products better, you reduce your documentation and customer service costs.

In short, don't always innovate to make things more complex, innovate to simplify. And remember KISS.

Lesson

Are Your Ideas Audacious Enough?

If you had been monitoring the ideas proposed at Supertrade over its history from innovative start-up to bureaucratic multinational, you would have noticed that over time, ideas have became less and less audacious. The founders wanted to change the world. Today, most people in the company are suggesting incremental improvements rather than radical ideas.

This is too bad. There tends to be a correlation between how audacious and risky an idea is and its innovativeness. Disruptive innovations – in other words, innovative ideas which disrupt industry and dramatically change a business sector – are inevitably audacious and highly risky. They are also highly innovative and, if they work as hoped, bring in huge rewards. However, do bear in mind that not every audacious idea is a potential disruptive innovation. Many are not, but a precious few are. If you do not welcome audacious ideas, you close your company's potential to launch disruptive innovations!

Consider Niklas Zennström and Janus Friis who developed their own voice over Internet protocol (VoIP). They devised a business – Skype - around it and offered easy, free telephone calls over the World Wide Web as well as dirt cheap calls from the Web to ordinary telephones. Their business model was audacious: a couple of Swedish guys take on the world's telephone service providers; it was innovative and it was risky. People might well have decided they were not ready for VoIP; they might not trust the system; or Internet Service Providers, who are often divisions of telecommunications companies offering telephony services, might have tried to prevent Skype calls. In which case, the two Swedish guys would have lost a lot of money.

In fact, Skype has taken off like a rocket. There are more than 100 million Skype users around the world and the two Swedish chaps sold their company to eBay for €1.9 billion (US$2.4 billion). Not bad for an audacious idea.

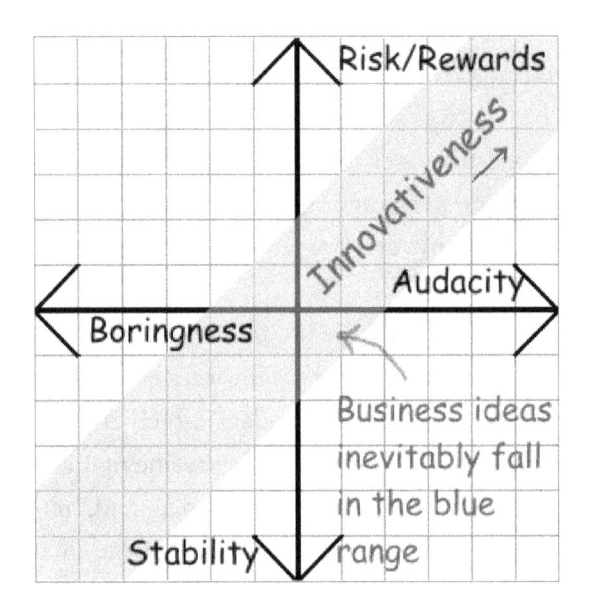

To visualise the importance of audaciousness in business innovation, look at the image above. The "innovativeness" bar, that runs diagonally up the chart, represents the range where most business ideas fall. Audacious business ideas are risky yet innovative. Boring business ideas are safe and not very risky. But they do not bring high rewards. Most business ideas, of course, tend to fall near the axis.

There are several useful things we can learn from this chart.

1. Although we in Europe and America tend to favour highly innovative ideas, it is clear that a handful of boring business ideas resulting in incremental innovation can also bring benefits to your organisation. Thus, you should not focus all your innovative efforts on big, disruptive innovation. You should also devote resources on capturing smaller, moderately innovative ideas and implementing them on a steady basis. A combination of occasional radical innovation and regular incremental innovation is the best balance.

2. As I have stated before, many companies have an overly strict idea review process that requires every idea pass a number of hurdles and committees before it is implemented. Very often these committees attempt to reduce the risk of the idea. That's understandable. They want to protect the company against risk. Often they want to protect their own jobs by not authorising a risky idea. Unfortunately, they are wrong. By reducing risk, they are also making an idea more boring, less innovative and reducing the potential reward.

3. Conversely, an idea can often be pushed to be more audacious, thus increasing its reward potential – but also its risk. Bear this in mind the next time you brainstorm ideas. When you get a few good ideas, don't stop there. Push the best ideas further. Actively try to make them more audacious.

4. If an idea is very boring and of low risk, its reward potential is also low. Thus you need to be certain that the cost of implementing the idea will not be greater than the rewards it brings in.

Conclusion

The next time you need to generate ideas, push for audacity. In an ideas campaign or brainstorming session, reward the most audacious ideas. When generating ideas solo, be audacious. The more, the better. After all, most companies are very good at toning down audacious ideas. Very few are good at pushing conservative ideas to be more audacious.

Phase 5

Realisation

Journey

Decisions

The new path meandered along to the extent it was sometimes hard to believe we were making any progress. But a glance down the mountain was all the evidence we needed that we had already covered a considerable part of our journey.

At one point, we passed a large plateau covered in grass, where a flock of sheep grazed lazily between the stone ruins of what had once been some kind of building. The sun shone off their rich woollen coats.

"What a beautiful sight," remarked Jane.

"Indeed it is," said I. "And an ancient one. According to the locals this family of sheep has been occupying this plateau for hundreds of years."

"Probably since those buildings were built," added Jane.

"Apparently. But there were more sheep a few generations ago. It seems the flock is slowly getting smaller over time," I explained.

Jane thought for a moment. "Unless something changes, these sheep's offspring and their offspring with graze this field for generations – much as they are now – until they all die out. Then there will be nothing."

"But the grass will grow longer, I expect. Or some other opportunistic animals may eventually occupy the field," I said.

As we passed the field, one of the sheep looked up at us and let out a sincere "baaah".

A half hour later we came to a fork in the path. "Let's check the map," said Jane.

We opened the map and looked at the options. On the path to the left, just a couple of hundred metres from the fork, was a lift that climbed the mountain. Next to it was a set of ladders and stairs that also led up the side of the mountain. Pointing to them, I explained, "I believe those pre-date the lift, but are still used for emergencies."

According to the map, the lift went up to the entrance to Wat Watanatahm, a Buddhist temple which was on the opposite side of the mountain and some distance down from our destination.

The path to the left was a continuation of our path. It wound its way along the mountain and would eventually take us to the front of the Temple of Ideas.

"What do you think?" I asked.

"Well, the lift would take us up a substantial chunk of the mountain relatively quickly, even if it is a slow lift," Said Jane. "But it's not clear how we would get from the Buddhist Temple to the Temple of Ideas."

She stopped to think for a moment, then continued. "The advantage to the left path is that it goes directly to the Temple. Based on what we have seen it should not be too demanding and the view is lovely. The disadvantage is that it will take a while to reach the temple. But we should make it by late afternoon at this rate.

"The advantage to the lift is that it gets us up the mountain a lot faster. But the going from the top, from Wat Watanatahm, is unclear. There are no obvious paths shown on the map, although there could be paths through here or here" she pointed to the map. "Or we might even be able to cut through the temple grounds. But it's just not sure.

"So, I reckon our best bet is to follow this path."

"Sounds good to me," I said and we pressed forward.

However, we had hardly walked 20 minutes or so when the quality of the path deteriorated rapidly. At points it was extremely muddy. Further on, where it hugged the edge of the mountain, bits of it had fallen away. Not surprisingly, our progress slowed considerably. Worse, it was clear that it was only going to get harder — at least as far as we could see. Indeed, some distance ahead, it looked as if a bridge spanning a gorge was in a very sad state of repair. I doubt either of us fancied taking our chances crossing it, which would have meant climbing down the gorge and back up again.

"This is getting ugly," I noted. It's far worse than last time I came this way.

"Indeed it is," said Jane.

Thinking a moment, she continued, "I hate to turn back as we've already spent a half hour coming this way and it will take us just as long to get back to the fork."

"Shall we push forward then?" I asked. "The path probably clears up further ahead."

"It's tempting," said Jane. But if it doesn't get better, we will still have to give up on this path, return to the fork and try the alternative. I'm not sure I want to invest any more time on this route."

"Very good," I said smiling inside. Jane was a quick learner and rational evaluator. She would clearly be an excellent innovation master.

We made our way back to the fork in the path, took the other route and found a lift car waiting for us. We stepped inside, push the button marked "Wat Watanatahm" and rode the lift slowly up the mountainside. In spite of the slight setback, we were making progress and I had no doubt that we'd make it to the Temple of Ideas in time for dinner.

Dialogue

Decisions, Decisions

The two company presidents meet up in an Antwerp bar that specialises in Belgian beers. Indeed, the sign out front boasts over 100 different beers on the menu. Alpha is puzzling over the menu.

Alpha: Lord love a duck, what a choice of beers. I'm not sure whether to go with something I know and like, such as a Duval or Chimay; or whether to try something new.

Beta: Go on, be daring. It's more in the spirit of innovation.

Alpha: Right you are. I'll try one of these Gueuze beers, then. This Girardin looks intriguing.

Beta: Excellent. I believe I'll try a bottle of Blanche de Namur.

Waiter: [Approaches table] Goeie dag…

Beta: Ah hello. May I have a bottle of Blanche de Namur and a bottle of the Girardin Gueze, please, young man?

Waiter: Of course sir. [walks away from table and towards bar]

Alpha: You know, at the old HQ, we've been doing a bit of that creative problem solving stuff you told me about at the

         Indian restaurant. It works a treat for generating useful ideas.

Beta: Doesn't it though?

Alpha: Indeed. Now the challenge is working out which ideas are best.

Beta: I don't think you should bandy around the word "best", when it comes to ideas. It's too vague, really.

Alpha: Really?

Beta: Yes, after all, you want to innovate don't you?

Alpha: Yes, of course.

The waiter brings two bottles of beer and two glasses, each custom designed for the accompanying beer. He opens the bottles and pours glasses. The two company presidents toast and take deep swigs.

Beta: Then you want to choose the ideas most likely to become innovations.

Alpha: Yes of course. And those are....

Beta: Creative ideas that add value to your company, old thing. You know, ideas that increase income or reduce costs or, best of all, do both.

Alpha: Of course! Is that not the same as the best ideas?

Beta: Until you define best as meaning most innovative, no. A Duval may be the best beer in Belgium – just as an example – but it's made by monks, for goodness sakes – and it's been made the same way for centuries.

Whereas a Gueze, like you have ordered, is a relatively modern innovation – at least in terms of beer. It combines Lambic beers – those are wheat beers going through some kind of spontaneous fermentation using special yeasts unique to the Pajottenland bit of Belgium – together with traditional beers. So, it may not be the best beer. But it was an innovation that helped a region of this little country to develop a unique beer industry.

Alpha: I see.

Beta: I thought you might.

Alpha: But I never knew you were an expert on Belgian beers. I always thought you to be more of a wine connoisseur, actually.

Beta: I am.

Alpha: Then where....

Beta: Reading the back of the menu while waiting for you.

Alpha: Ahhh. Yes, sorry I was late.

Beta: No worries. It's a fascinating menu, I recommend it!

Alpha: I'll add it to my reading list.

Meanwhile, about selecting the best... Sorry, most innovative ideas.

Beta: Well, the thing you need to do is not try and guess which ideas are the best. Rather you need to determine which ideas meet the relevant criteria that you use to judge them.

Alpha: Ah. And the criteria?

Beta: You should have worked those out in the innovation plan you and your team prepared.

Alpha: Yes, of course. I forgot. It's been a busy week, you know.

Beta: I know. So, it's worth your while popping back and reviewing that bit of the plan. Indeed, it's worth your while to develop a policy for reviewing and implementing ideas.

Alpha: I was thinking I ought to.

Beta: Good on you. According to my Innovation Master, a lot of innovation processes break down at this stage, favouring small innovations over bigger ones, killing good ideas before they can be implemented and then letting mediocre ideas fester and waste stacks of money.

Alpha: I see. And I suppose you are going to tell me that if I want to know more, I should read on.

Beta: Of course! But let's have another beer first, eh?

Alpha: Now that is a good idea!

Beta: Thanks.

Lesson

Evaluation and Implementation

If you have succeeded in your initial tasks as an Innovation Master you will not only have motivated your people to be creative and hence innovative, but you will also have created a machine which generates lots of ideas. You now face the challenge of evaluating, testing and implementing the ideas which have the greatest innovation potential (remember: we define corporate innovation as the *implementation* of creative ideas in order to generate value for the company).

As Beta notes, it is not enough simply to choose the "best ideas" and then run with them. Ideas with the greatest potential may initially seem absurd or non-viable. They may even scare your colleagues who could fear that the implementation of radical ideas will threaten their jobs.

"Best ideas", however, tend to be incremental innovations: useful, but not necessarily exciting. Absurd ideas may be brilliant or they may indeed be absurd. As a result, a structured evaluation process is essential for providing managers with the information they need in order to make intelligent decisions about which ideas to implement.

Even so, as Jane and I found after following what seemed to the best path to the temple of ideas, seeming good ideas may turn out not to work as planned. The Innovation Master realises that highly creative ideas are risky and may not work out. Hence, a process needs to be in place for determining when an idea is not working so that its implementation may be cancelled and resources can be redirected towards the implementation of other ideas with innovation potential.

But we are getting ahead of ourselves here. The first thing the Innovation Master needs is a functional and efficient evaluation process. Such a process will probably involve several steps which must meet these criteria:

- identify the ideas that are most likely to succeed as innovations for the company.

- ensure that complex ideas are reviewed by people with the appropriate expertise necessary to understand what would be necessary to implement the idea – and what might go wrong.

- enable a middle manager to defend the idea to senior management, stakeholders, and financial officers who may need to grant budgetary approval of the idea.

- make it possible to review a large number of ideas in a resource-efficient manner.

- improve the idea by identifying potential implementation problems and preparing suitable actions to overcome those problems. Sadly, this last aspect is often lost in formal idea review procedures.

Methods

There are all kinds of idea review methods. We will look at three methods that we use: quick and dirty elimination, evaluation matrices and SWOT analysis.

Quick and Dirty Elimination

A good brainstorming event can easily generate 50 or 100 ideas. An ideas campaign in a large enterprise can generate many more. As a result, the initial idea review is what we might call a quick and dirty elimination round (Q&DER) – what you might also call a pass-fail evaluation – in which a team of evaluators read each idea. They quickly decide which ideas to retain for further evaluation and development and which ideas to dispose of immediately.

Unfortunately, there are two innovation threats in such Q&DERs:

1. Lack of defined criteria for determining which ideas should be retained and which should be eliminated.
2. Not considering obvious methods of counteracting the weaknesses that cause an idea to be eliminated.

Lack of Defined Criteria

Whenever people are reviewing a list of ideas for viability, they have some criteria in their minds. In a business environment, these criteria are likely to include budget, saleability, time-frames and the like. However, if the criteria are left unspoken, there are two dangers:

1. If there are multiple reviewers, they may have differing criteria sets in their minds. As a result, ideas are subject to a harsher first analysis which is overly likely to see off potentially good ideas. Imagine there are four evaluators each with three differing criteria on their minds. As a result, any idea would need to pass all 12 criteria (4 evaluators x 3 criteria each) in order to be considered for further analysis. And that further analysis might well be less rigorous than the Q&DER!
2. One or more reviewers may have inappropriate criteria in mind. For instance, imagine an ideas campaign seeking new product solutions. Senior management may not care so much about the cost of implementing the ideas as they do about the return on investment (RoI) of the ideas. However, if evaluators are eliminating ideas they believe are too expensive, they

may kill off potential new product ideas that offer tremendous RoI, albeit for a high initial investment.

Fortunately, the solution to this problem is obvious: clarify your elimination criteria prior to the Q&DER. Moreover, ensure that anyone involved in the Q&DER is clear about the criteria.

Counteracting Obvious Weaknesses in Ideas
Imagine you are part of a team evaluating new software ideas for mobile telephones. You generate a lot of ideas and need to do a Q&DER. Your Q&DER criterion is that ideas should be viable on a standard mobile telephone unit. Here are some of the ideas:

- Notepad for making notes.
- Application for finding friends in the area.
- E-book application so people can read books.
- Possibility to control heating/cooling devices in your home

Chances are you would dismiss the e-book application idea as being non-viable. After all telephone screens are too small to display more than a few words, resolution is poor and it would be irritating to have to scroll through an entire book.

But what about audio books? They form a huge and growing market. Friends of mine who commute by car to work listen to audio books on their car CD players. Would it not be even more convenient to carry the audio book in a telephone so that the user could listen to it whenever she has some spare time - and not just in her car?

Surely, then, the book application deserves a more thorough evaluation. But it would be unlikely to get that evaluation in an elimination round - particularly if there are 100 ideas to consider.

Even the Best Criteria Sets Are Not Perfect

In this example, there was nothing wrong with the Q&DER criterion. The problem was that the idea - as originally stated - did not meet the criterion. However, with only minor modification the idea would have passed.

In fact, such elimination of potentially viable ideas happens frequently, not only in quick and dirty reviews but also in formal evaluations simply because evaluators see their roles as being exclusively that of critics.

But they are not critics. Indeed, can you imagine having a team in your company called the "Idea Criticism Committee"? Of course not. Evaluators are evaluators - that's why we call them that!

Again, the solution to the problem is simple. Rather than simply reviewing ideas on a pass-fail basis, evaluators in the Q&DER should review each idea following three simple steps:

1. Does it meet the criteria? If so, it passes.
2. If not, MIGHT there be a way to change the failing point(s) so that it meets the criteria? If so, it passes.
3. If the idea fails both of the above, it is eliminated.

And the final rule of quick and dirty idea reviews is: if you are not sure whether or not an idea can be made to pass a criteria set, don't eliminate it. Once an idea is eliminated, it is quickly forgotten. On the other hand, if it does not pass a more structured evaluation later, the questionable idea can still be eliminated at that time.

Evaluation Matrix

The evaluation matrix, as has been covered previously, is a simple array in which experts compare an idea with a set of criteria. In our experience, five criteria are best as it allows for a rounded review without bogging down the evaluators in unnecessary detail. The evaluator ranks how well the idea meets each criterion (we use a scale of 0-5 points for each criterion). Evaluators are also encouraged to provide comments elaborating on their ratings and, in particular, suggesting how the idea might be improved to overcome weaknesses.

The evaluation matrix provides a criterion by criterion score, as well as an overall score for each idea. Assuming several ideas, focusing on a particular problem or business issue, are being evaluated at the same time, these scores can be compared and the highest scoring ideas can be selected for further review. However, it is important to look at the evaluators' comments. An idea with a low score might be vastly improved following minor changes.

I favour the evaluation matrix as the primary idea review approach because it is simple to set up, requires a minimum amount of time for review, enables comparative idea review and makes it easy to identify the most promising ideas in a large collection of ideas. That said, the evaluation matrix in itself is not usually sufficient for making a final decision on an idea that may cost millions of Euro to implement. But it helps you select ideas for more detailed review, thus making the review process more efficient.

SWOT Analysis
An analysis of Strengths, Weaknesses, Opportunities and Threats (SWOT) is an old marketing stand-by and as such is a useful follow up to an evaluation matrix. In the unlikely event you are unfamiliar with SWOT analysis, it is a simple form in which reviewers indicate the potential strengths, weaknesses, opportunities and threats of an idea. Because the SWOT analysis looks at an idea from different perspectives, it provides a more rounded review of an idea than some methods.

I like to use a SWOT analysis approach that includes a scoring system in which reviewers give 0 to 5 points each for strengths and opportunities and takes away 0 to 5 points each for weaknesses and threats. This provides a SWOT metric which can be handy for comparing large numbers of ideas.

I also ask evaluators to suggest methods to overcome weaknesses and threats.

Idea Trials

If you are evaluating high-value ideas, that is ideas that will require substantial investment, will require substantial changes or which involve significant risk, why not put those ideas to trial by jury? This is a unique, but creative approach that gives your idea champions and critics an opportunity to put promising creative ideas to the test. Idea trials are conceptually simple.

Assign each idea to a person or team who will act as that idea's advocate. The advocate's job is to analyse the idea thoroughly and be prepared to defend the idea. The advocate should look at strengths, weaknesses, opportunities and threats, and determine how to strengthen weaknesses and overcome threats.

Meanwhile, an evaluation team is charged with being a team of judges. Potentially, you might even bring others to act as a jury.

Advocates are given time to prepare their cases. The judges are given time to prepare their questioning.

Then you create an idea courtroom where each advocate presents her case and answers the judge's questions. If ideas are competing for budget, you could even allow idea advocates to question each other. In the end, each advocate concludes her case. The judges adjourn and make their recommendations. Of course the recommendations might not be quite so clear cut as in the courtroom: "Your honour, we find the idea guilty!" The judges might decide to combine ideas, implement parts of an idea or insist one or more advocates go back and develop aspects of their ideas further.

While idea trials are more time and resource consuming than traditional evaluation methods, this approach guarantees an in-depth analysis of each idea in a dynamic setting.

Idea Development

Once an idea passes these initial hurdles, it may be ready for implementation or it may require more detailed testing. We call this phase of idea review: "idea development" as it is no longer a process of evaluating an idea so much as a method to develop it for implementation.

Idea development may include business case preparation, prototype development, project management initiation, test marketing or any other process that takes an idea from concept to implementation. Moreover, how a firm develops an idea depends on the nature of the idea, the nature of the firm and existing processes for implementing ideas.

Criticism versus Improvement

Over the years, I have noticed that business analysts tend to be overly critical of new ideas. This is also understandable as they are tasked with managing and minimising risk. And creative ideas tend to be the riskiest. As a result, many evaluators stress weaknesses and threats. On one hand, this is understandable. Your company should not be implementing ideas that will prove to be costly failures. But, many weaknesses can readily be improved. An idea that would be very expensive to implement may, with minor changes, be implemented at far lower cost. And by improving a creative idea's weaknesses, you may be turning a costly failure into a profitable success!

Evaluation Teams

Evaluations should be performed by a team of people with relevant expertise. Ideally, that expertise should be varied. For instance, if you are evaluating new product ideas for an electronic gadget, your experts might include engineers, marketing people, retailers (who would sell the product) and one or more people representative of the consumers expected to buy the new products.

Evaluator Agendas and Prejudices

A particular benefit to having teams review ideas is that while individual evaluators are prejudiced, a varied team is likely to cancel such prejudices out.

For example: an engineer trained in an older technology may well be reluctant to give a high evaluation score to an idea that uses a new technology with which she is not familiar. The success of such an idea might well threaten her job! A jealous manager might not like the fact that her subordinates are more creative than her and so might give poor evaluation scores to creative ideas. At the other end of the spectrum, creativity and innovation people like you and I are often too enthusiastic about the most creative ideas and so give overly high scores for creativity. Sometimes, a less creative idea might prove to be the more innovative (in terms of being profitable).

Too Many Evaluators Spoil the Idea

Just as too many cooks spoil the broth, too many evaluators are equally likely to spoil a creative idea.

When I talk to larger organisations (2000+ people) that are developing innovation processes, a lot of them set up very rigid multiple evaluation procedures for implementing an idea. Typically, if an idea is identified as having potential, it goes through a preliminary evaluation. Provided the evaluation is successful, it goes through a more rigid evaluation and a then a final evaluation. Ideas – together with a critique – which do not make it through an evaluation, are often sent back to the person responsible for the idea. She can then improve the idea and re-submit it for re-evaluation.

Such a structure is fine if you are limiting your innovation to incremental innovation; but deadly for radical innovation. That's because evaluation is largely about risk control. Once you get too many people looking for potential risk in a creative idea, you can be sure they will find a lot of risk – too much risk to their minds. Thus the most creative ideas are likely to be sent back with comments like: "Try to make this fit better with our current product line"; "Such big changes in our operations are likely to cause disruption, please scale back your ideas to fit better with our current methods"; "That does not fit in with our business model."

Rarely does an idea receive a critique such as: "That's a crazy idea, but we believe you can make it even crazier. Go for it!"; "That idea is so radical it will redefine the market. But let's see if we can push it even further. After all, there's no point in being radical unless you are going to push your ideas to the limit"; "Albert Einstein once said 'If at first the idea is not absurd, then there is no hope for it.' Your idea is not absurd enough yet. Push it further."

Of course large companies need to be careful about risk. After all, if an idea could "make or break" your company, you do have to bear in mind the "break" potential.

On the other hand, one major reason why small companies tend to be more innovative than large companies is because the latter often require that ideas undergo multiple evaluations prior to implementation. In small companies, there is usually a single decision-maker who can readily say "Let's do it" to an idea.

This is not to say that large companies should do away with their structured evaluation process. In the case of an idea that will not bring about major innovation, evaluations are useful for determining whether or not that idea is likely to succeed and where its weaknesses are. This is important.

But, large companies should have a fast track to implementation for radical ideas which division managers believe have the potential to boost income substantially – even if they also believe those same ideas have the potential to cost the company a fortune if they do not work.

When an idea goes to the fast track, a very small team should review the idea and determine how to implement the idea while minimising risk; such as by launching the product concept in one market initially, testing the operational overhaul in a single office or building a prototype and taking it to the dealers.. Sometimes, however, the idea will be so radical that the best move will be to implement immediately, before your competition has the same idea.

It is important that any risk reduction action should aim to reduce risk in the event of failure rather than to dilute the innovativeness of the idea. One way to do this is provide division managers with discretionary budgets for high risk, innovative projects.

But why stop at adding a fast track to implementation? Why not provide flexible evaluation of ideas? Thus normal ideas would go through a highly structured evaluation process. Radical ideas would take a fast track approach. Hot ideas would undergo a single evaluation and so on.

In other words, taking an innovative approach to evaluation can lead to successful implementation of more innovative ideas. And that's what innovation is all about, isn't it?

Lesson

When to Kill an Idea

As an Innovation Master, one of your less pleasant but necessary duties is killing ideas. You will understand that the creative process results in the generation of more ideas than your organisation can viably implement. So, some of those ideas will have to die. You also know that the problem most people and organisations have is that they tend to kill ideas at the wrong times – either too early or too late – and this is very detrimental to their innovation process.

In fact, most ideas are killed way, way too early. Consider the following exchange, variations of which can be heard daily in corporate corridors around the world:

Sam: I was just thinking. If we added wi-fi connectivity to our scanners, our customers...

Martha: You must be joking! It would add to costs and what reasons would shoppers possibly have for connecting wirelessly to the web?

Sam: Well, I thought...

Martha: I'm sorry, I'm on my way to a meeting now. I trust the financial projections for the next quarter will be on my desk by the end of business today!

In just a few seconds, Managing Martha has killed an idea without even trying to understand it. Worse, if she does this a couple more times, she will essentially communicate to Sam and others that she does not welcome ideas. And they will learn to keep ideas to themselves. Sadly, this happens all the time in all but the most innovation-enlightened companies.

Idea Generation or Extermination Actions?
Sadly, even when organisations purposely attempt to generate creative ideas, such as through brainstorming events, suggestion schemes and other activities, they often kill ideas off too early. Sometimes they even kill ideas during the idea generation activities.

A worst case example was told to me by a manager of a global engineering firm. She explained how the company had set up a suggestion scheme to solicit ideas from employees. Moreover, they decided that it was critical to give idea submitters feedback as soon as possible in order to demonstrate that they were acting on all ideas received. Every idea was evaluated within a couple of weeks of submission and a report sent to the submitter.

Like most suggestion schemes, this one did not use ideas campaigns to focus creative thinking on specific business needs. As a result, all kinds of ideas came in. Most of them, of course, were unrelated to current business needs. Many were not even related to the company's business at all! Following policy, idea submitters promptly received rejection notices.

In no time, staff worked out that submitting an idea to the suggestion scheme was a sure-fire method of getting a critical idea rejection notice and, not surprisingly, the initiative died within weeks of its kick-off.

This same problem plagues many poorly facilitated brainstorming events, where participants, and particularly senior manager participants, criticise ideas during the idea generation. Other participants quickly learn that wild ideas are going to be criticised and learn to keep their creativity to themselves.

Poor Evaluation Process Kills Promising Ideas too Quickly

If ideas make it past the creative idea generation process, the next step is to evaluate them in order to determine how well they meet corporate needs. In theory, this is a good time to kill ideas. You have generated a lot of ideas and now you need to select the best. This is normally done via some kind of evaluation process in which the idea is compared to one or more criteria for viability.

The danger here is that sometimes ideas might not initially meet a critical criterion. But with some modification, those ideas can be made to meet the criterion. For instance, you might be reviewing a number of ideas to determine which ones could be implemented on a budget of $1 million. A particularly clever idea may, on first instance, seem to need a budget of twice that to implement. As a result, the idea is likely to be killed.

But, if the reviewers had asked themselves, "How might we do the same thing at half the cost?", they might not only have found a solution, but they might have made the idea even better.

Five Criteria Are Best

As I have stressed in this book, it is always better to evaluate particularly promising ideas against a five criteria matrix. If an idea fails on one criterion, but scores highly on the others it will still have a relatively high score and remain in consideration for implementation.

In addition, if you are truly keen on high-level innovation, you should always earmark the craziest, most outlandish and most creative ideas for further consideration. Such ideas may fail your regular evaluation tests because they are so unusual. You may have to create special evaluations to determine their viability.

In summary, ideas have a difficult birth and precious few actually survive to become projects – arguably the next stage in idea development. But when they do become projects, they become almost indestructible!

Indestructible Projects

Unlike an idea, a project requires people to manage it. It requires a budget and should have clear goals. As the project develops, the people running it often establish an emotional attachment to it. Moreover, they realise that the project's failure might at best be damaging to their reputations and at worst be detrimental to their futures in the firm. The failure of a large project could result in people losing their jobs and corporate loss of face.

The result is, once an idea becomes a project, the people behind it are unlikely to want to kill it – no matter how bad the results are. To make matters worse, the longer project managers keep a bad project going, the greater the consequences of failure: more money is wasted, more people are affected and more damage is done to reputations. So, ironically, the worse a project becomes, the harder it becomes for those behind it to kill the project.

This has consequences. As budget and resources are being sucked up by a once promising idea that has become a bad project, there is less budget and resources for other promising ideas.

This, in fact, ruined many e-businesses that were devised during the dot-com boom of the late 1990s. Many had good, creative ideas behind them, but those ideas turned bad in their implementations. Sadly, rather than killing off bad ideas early on, managers sought – and often found – more venture capital to throw at their ideas, making their failures even more spectacular.

Boo.com, a UK based on-line fashion retailer that went bust in 2000, blew over £80 million on developing a very innovative, cutting edge web site that included a virtual assistant and Flash-based tools for displaying garments. Sadly, these tools sucked bandwidth at a time when most consumers were connecting to the Internet with slow dial-up modems. Worse, usability was appalling.

As Boo.com failed, managers did not dump the innovative tools and try alternative approaches. Rather they threw more money at the tools and marketing. In the end, Boo made history but few sales.

Establish a Balance of Idea Killing

Clearly, what organisations need to do is to allow more ideas to live longer during the early idea generation and incubation stage. Indeed, more ideas should become projects. But, those projects need to have very clear milestones which must be reached at an early stage of the project. If those milestones are not reached, the project should be quietly killed and resources applied to a new project.

Likewise, managers behind projects should not be reprimanded if their projects do not reach early milestones. Rather, they should be rewarded for being sensible and encouraged to share their learnings with their colleagues in order to prevent similar failures in the future.

And then, of course, they should be given newly incubated projects to work on.

Lesson

What's Your Plan B?

"Plan B" is a term that refers to a secondary plan to put into action in the event the primary plan (Plan A) does not work out. It is also the name of various medications, at least two music groups, a magazine and several organisations. But the Innovation Master is primarily interested in the original meaning of the term.

As we know by now, the implementation of a highly innovative new idea is a risky endeavour. If the idea works out, it is highly profitable, tends to make employees feel good about their firm, makes stakeholders happy and often generates good press, all of which is great.

But, if it fails, the same idea will at the least result in lost income. In innovation-unfriendly companies, the failed idea can have far more serious consequences, such as reprimands for those responsible for launching the idea, loss of jobs and restrictions to launching creative projects in the future.

However, as we have noted, a more frequent problem with highly innovative ideas is that they are not given the opportunity to fail! One way to make dealing with a failed idea more palatable is by preparing an alternative.

This Is Where Plan B Comes in
Whether you have to present a radical idea to a committee or simply put it into action yourself, having a plan B is a great way to mitigate risk. Plan B will probably be less innovative than plan A. It should be

designed to minimise financial or reputation damage that could result from a failed plan A.

For instance, if you plan to introduce a radical new product, plan B might involve reducing production quantities of the new product if certain targets are not met. Those production facilities could then be re-organised to manufacture another product.

Being Creative with Plan B
Even though your plan B may be intended to be less radical than plan A, you should use the same innovation process methods for developing plan B as you would for plan A. This would probably involve running ideas campaigns on "In what ways might plan A fail?" These ideas can be evaluated for likelihood and consequences. Those ideas which are perceived as real threats can be combined into categories and form the basis for one or more ideas campaigns designed to identify plan B options.

However, when evaluating plan B ideas, you should give high marks to low risk ideas, even if they are not very exciting. Remember, the point of plan B is to have a safe alternative if plan A does not work.

Two Outcomes
If you are creative with your plan B development, one of two things may happen.

At the very least, you can present your plan B as an escape route to be implemented should plan A not work. This can demonstrate that in spite of the potential risk of plan A, you have allowed for failure and can implement an alternative plan that will minimise financial loss. Of course, if you are a decision maker yourself, you can feel more confident about launching a highly innovative new concept, knowing that you have a fall-back in the event things do not work to expectation.

On the other hand, you may find that in looking for a plan B, you actually develop a concept that is even better than your plan A! In this case, you may decide to drop plan A and run with plan B instead.

Not every idea needs a plan B. But if you are implementing a highly innovative idea whose failure could have substantial unpleasant consequences for your firm, you really should have a plan B. And perhaps even a plan C!

Lesson

Idea Voting Doesn't Work

One of the most pervasively flawed concepts in organisational innovation is that voting for ideas is a good idea. The Innovation Master knows that the opposite is true. Voting is a completely ineffective method of identifying potentially innovative ideas. Worse, it tends to hide the most innovative ideas and so can actually work against your innovation process.

With the growth of interest in innovation, a number of firms have recently launched suggestion scheme software products. These products make it easy for employees (in closed systems) or even the public (in open systems) to submit ideas about anything. The great thing about such suggestion scheme software is that, properly promoted, they can generate 1000s of varied ideas. The bad thing about such suggestion schemes is that, properly promoted, they can generate 1000s of varied ideas! After all, if you actually want to innovate, you have to devote resources to reviewing those 1000s of ideas in order to identify which ideas might become innovations. And without a structured innovation process behind the suggestion scheme, each idea needs to be individually reviewed.

Not long ago, in an unknown software company somewhere in the world, some bright spark had the idea to add a voting system to their suggestion scheme software product. On the surface, the logic seems good: with so many ideas coming into the suggestion scheme, why not let users of the system vote on ideas in order to identify the best ideas? Clearly the ideas with the most votes will be the best, after all they will have been elected following proper democratic due process. Then the owners of the system need only implement the ideas with the most votes and innovate like crazy.

There are two flaws with this seemingly lovely theory. Firstly, research in social psychological behaviour, group motivation and incentives demonstrate that the theory is completely wrong. Secondly, no one seems to have actually read up on the research and, as a result, nearly every suggestion scheme software company uses the same highly flawed voting system.

Let's look at the flaws.

People Do Not Vote on Best Ideas. They Follow Trends
Research has shown that in transparent systems where people can vote on submissions, their voting is based more on trends than on the quality of the actual submissions. Particularly interesting and relevant is a recent study by Matthew Salganik, Peter Dodds, and Duncan Watts, entitled "Experimental Study of Inequality and Unpredictability in an Artificial Cultural Market."[1]

The researchers had 14,000 volunteers participate in a web-based music download system. Participants were able to listen to songs from obscure bands, vote on how much they liked the songs and then download those songs.

Users were divided into groups. In the control group, users could not observe the actions of other users. They simply listened, voted and downloaded. The remaining users were divided into eight parallel worlds, each using an interface available only to other members in the same parallel world. In each of these worlds, participants could see which songs other members of their world had downloaded and watch the voting in real time.

In each group, a strikingly different collection of musical tracks was voted in as best. In the control group, the top choices were spread widely, with no one track getting a huge number of votes. And this was assumed to represent participants' actual liking of individual musical tracks.

In each of the worlds in which users could watch the voting results, something interesting happened. Users first listened to the tracks which had the most votes. In many instances, they also voted for these tracks and downloaded them. Moreover, they often did not even bother to listen to the tracks with no votes. This created a snowball effect, with a small number of tracks getting a high number of votes and many other tracks ignored.

Most interestingly, the top-voted songs in each of the worlds were very different from one world to the next. Indeed, economists have long noted that this "network effect" occurs within populations.

Think About It

If you stop and think about your own behaviour, you will see that this makes sense. Imagine you visit a suggestion scheme for the first time. You see that there are 100s or 1000s or more ideas in the system. Although the ideas are categorised, there is no logical order to them. Most likely you will initially look at the ideas with the most votes, assuming that these are the better ideas. And, if you like the ideas, you will vote in their favour. You probably will not want to admit it, but you will also very likely assume that highly voted ideas must be good in order to have achieved their high scores. As a result, you will push up the popularity of the popular ideas but are unlikely to even have the time to look at the unpopular ideas.

If 100s of people behave similarly, it is no surprise that those ideas, which are submitted early and receive a few positive votes, quickly become the most popular. However, the most popular ideas are not necessarily those that have the greatest innovation potential. Indeed, if you look at typical behaviour in a brainstorming or other ideation event, you will realise that they are unlikely to be the most creative ideas. And remember, it is the highly creative ideas that are most likely to become breakthrough innovations.

Creative Ideas Come Last

If you have ever participated in a brainstorming exercise, you will know that the first ideas tend to be the obvious ones. By definition, then, they are not particularly creative and are unlikely to become breakthrough innovations. It is only after the obvious ideas have been exhausted that people start pushing their minds and being creative.

However, as we have seen, in an on-line system with popular voting, the first ideas are likely to capture the votes. As a result, more visitors will look at them and fewer will look at the latter, ideas which will not receive many votes. However, it is among those unpopular ideas that the most creative are likely to sit!

So, it is clear that voting in suggestion schemes does not identify the most creative ideas and may even act to hide those ideas. But it gets worse!

Topic Fixation

Topic fixation is a danger in any kind of brainstorming activity. In traditional brainstorming, it occurs when an individual suggests an idea that other brainstormers like. As a result, they suggest similar ideas and, as a result, you see a large number of very similar ideas being submitted with the further consequence that participants are not exploring other themes for ideas. This has been demonstrated empirically since the 1950s.

However, more recent research has shown that this happens in on-line systems too. Nicholas Kohn and Steven Smith of The University of Texas at Arlington, USA recently published a paper on "Collaborative Fixation: Effects of Others' Ideas on Brainstorming"[2]. Rather than looking at traditional brainstorming in a conference room, the researchers put volunteers in front of computers and had them suggest ideas using AOL instant messaging software. In other words, they submitted ideas on-line. Mr. Kohn found that "Fixation to other people's ideas can occur unconsciously and lead to you suggesting ideas that mimic your brainstorming partners'. Thus, you potentially become less creative."

While this research used small groups and did not include voting, it would seem likely that voting for or against ideas would encourage topic fixation. After all, if an idea gets a lot of votes in a suggestion scheme, users are likely to assume that such ideas are best and will want to submit similar ideas – not realising that the best ideas received their votes as a result of the network effect rather than because they are actually the best.

I have not yet come across research on this precise scenario. But, if you look at popular public suggestion schemes, you can certainly see not just similar ideas, but nearly identical ideas being submitted again and again and again. And this only adds to the workload of the administrators!

Conclusion

So, we can see that voting for ideas in suggestion scheme software encourages people to vote for ideas that achieve early popularity, usually for no better reason than that they were the first submitted ideas. Moreover, new visitors are likely to view only those ideas with the most votes, thereby being less likely to see, let alone vote on, more recently submitted ideas that are actually more creative (as a side note, most suggestion scheme software products do not identify how you should vote and those that do suggest you vote for the best ideas – see note above – rather than the most creative or the most unique). Finally, voting is likely, but admittedly unproven, to encourage topic fixation and result in a lot of duplicate and very similar ideas.

For administrators of suggestion scheme software, it is clear that voting will not make their jobs any easier. For submitters who know their ideas are more creative, but find their ideas are ignored, the result is likely to be frustration with the software and the suggestion scheme itself. Finally, users who see no correlation between votes and implementation – or who wonder why their popular ideas are ignored by administrators – are also likely to be frustrated and demotivated

In summary, voting is actually highly detrimental to suggestion schemes. If you wish to have some kind of user interaction on quality, however, there are two approaches you can take. Firstly, rather than popular voting, use a sliding scale such as Amazon uses with book reviews. Users on Amazon can give between one and five stars depending on how good a book is. Moreover, ratings are based on the number of stars and not the number of votes. Secondly clarify that stars should be awarded for creativity, uniqueness, added value or a similar attribute that is relevant to innovation potential. While these simple actions cannot replace a structured evaluation of ideas, they at least make the user interaction more relevant to the aims of the suggestion scheme.

References

1. Matthew J. Salganik, Peter Sheridan Dodds, Duncan J. Watts (2006) "Experimental Study of Inequality and Unpredictability in an Artificial Cultural Market" **Science** 311, 854 ; DOI: 10.1126/science.1121066
(http://www.sciencemag.org/cgi/reprint/311/5762/854.pdf -- PDF document)

2. Nicholas W. Kohn and Steven M. Smith (2010) "Collaborative Fixation: Effects of Others' Ideas on Brainstorming" **Applied Cognitive Psychology,** 29 March 2010
(http://www3.interscience.wiley.com/journal/123329584/abstract?CRETRY=1&SRETRY=0)

Lesson

Selling Ideas Up the Corporate Ladder

Unless you are both Innovation Master and CEO of your company, one major challenge you face is selling potentially innovative ideas up the corporate ladder to the people who are empowered to authorise the implementation of those ideas. Sadly, the more creative an idea is, the harder it is to convince managers to give you the okay to implement it.

This is ironic. If CEOS really wanted their firms to be innovative, you would think they would make it easy for employees to propose ideas to managers and easy for managers to propose ideas to senior managers and so on. Sadly, this seems rarely to be the case.

Of course, a structured idea management process can facilitate the communication of ideas as well as the evaluation and pre-implementation of those ideas. Provided senior management is behind the idea management process, this is a very effective way of selling ideas up the corporate ladder.

However, if your firm has not got an idea management process or top management is not behind the process, then selling ideas up the corporate ladder can be a challenge.

Prototyping

Ideas, of course, are harder to sell than material goods. If you can hand an item to someone, it is much easier to sell the person on the benefits of that item than it is if you simply describe the item. For this reason, the best way to sell an idea is to make a prototype of it – if at all possible.

If your idea is for a new product or improvements of an existing product, making a prototype is relatively easy. Using what tools you have available, you put together the best model of your idea possible. At the very least, computer generated images, drawings or even rough sketches can give your boss a clearer image of your product idea than mere words can. But, if you can build something your boss can touch and feel, it will become so much easier to sell your idea to her.

Prototyping Services

If your idea is for a new service that your firm could offer, prototyping becomes more difficult – but not impossible. You simply need to apply your creativity to the problem of how to prototype a service. For example, if your idea is a new consulting service your firm might offer, you could provide a short sample consultation to your direct report. If that's not feasible, you could perform a role-play of your service, with you and your colleagues playing the roles of service providers as well as customers. Better still, invite your superiors to play the role of the customers in order to give them a flavour of the advantages your service idea offers.

Admittedly, convincing your superiors to participate in a role-play, or even to watch a role-play, may not be easy. Thus you would probably do better to invite them to a new product idea meeting rather than invite them to participate in a role-play. Initially, they may not like the surprise, but if your idea is good enough, they will be impressed both by the idea and your innovative approach in presenting it.

Making a prototype of an operational idea is the most difficult of all, particularly if the idea is about changing a process. I have had success in drawing cartoons to show processes – the Corporate Innovation Machine illustration (page 41) is an example of my work!

Alternatively, it can sometimes be effective to make a prototype of a bad process in order to demonstrate the importance of replacing the process with a better one.

A Story

There is story, probably apocryphal, about an advertising agency making a pitch to British Rail (BR) in the 1970s or thereabouts. According to the story, the CEO and a number of other top people from British Rail were invited to an advertising agency to receive a pitch (advertising agency language for a business proposal) for the railway's advertising business.

When the BR team arrived at the agency, they were met by a disinterested receptionist sitting at her desk, reading a magazine and smoking a cigarette. She made them wait until she finished the article before rudely waving the BR executives to a waiting room which was small, smelly and lacked enough chairs for everyone. A table held a hot water machine, a lot of dirty cups, overflowing ashtrays and rubbish. The tea provided was terrible.

The BR people waited 20 minutes for the ad agency people to arrive. They didn't and the BR team got fed up and started to walk out. Just then, the CEO of the ad agency jumped out and said: "This is how your customers perceive British Rail's service. We intend to change that for you." The Adman proceeded to explain how his company would help improve BR's terrible image. Supposedly, the agency was hired on the spot.

Anyone who experienced BR in the 1970s will completely understand the story.

Whether or not the story is true, it is certainly a wonderful example of prototyping – or demonstrating – a very bad process in order to make people understand why the process needs improving, and making your superiors more receptive to your ideas about improving the process.

There are many, many ways to prototype an idea. The more creative your approach, the more likely you are to sell your creative idea up the ladder.

Lesson

Experimentation

Scientists and technologists, like Jane, who are involved in research tend to get Creative Problem Solving (see lesson on Creative Problem Solving) immediately. That is because the experimentation process used in scientific and technological research is very similar in process. Moreover, since new product, packaging and other innovations often come out of the Research and Development (R&D) divisions of most companies, the Innovation Master should also understand how experimentation works and how it can be used in non R&D innovation activities.

Experimentation is a wonderful means of playing with ideas and innovating. "Wait a minute, Jeffrey," you are probably thinking to yourself, "a chemist can experiment by mixing chemicals together and analysing the results. How can a human resources professional experiment? Genetic engineering of the staff?"

In fact there are a number of possibilities. The human resources (HR) manager can try out ideas on small groups of staff – such as populations of individual departments or offices. For example, if the HR manager wants to test the effects of flexitime (allowing staff to be flexible about what hours they work provided they work a minimum number of hours per week), she can have several different departments try out different forms of flexitime. One department might use a rigid software tool to time everyone's schedule to the minute, another might be given freedom to work when and how they please provided certain targets are met. Another department may have only a small amount of flexibility. And another may have significantly more flexibility. After a couple of weeks, the HR manager can analyse the results by talking to the employees, their division managers and attempting to measure productivity, work satisfaction and other factors. She can then tweak each group's flexitime structure, re-experiment and re-analyse the results over time.

In addition, creating models, building prototypes and drawing concepts on paper can all be effective means of experimentation. Operational people can often play with ideas by cutting out bits of paper to represent people, equipment, divisions, customers, actions and so on. By moving the paper around to represent different workflow possibilities, it is possible to experiment with ideas surprisingly effectively. If, like me, you think three dimensionally rather than two dimensionally, use children's building blocks or Lego building bricks to build models.

Sales and marketing people can experiment through role play, using actual customers, other employees or even acting students from the local university, to act as the customer while the sales or marketing people experiment with new ideas.

The important thing to bear in mind when experimenting is to push ideas as far as you can. If an idea seems to work in experimentation, don't stop. Push the idea further.

Finally: don't be afraid to try out radical ideas based on hunches. After all, that is where the best ideas often originate.

Lesson

Concept, Prototype, Production

The car industry has a long history of producing radical concept cars which they show off at motor shows. Concept cars tend to be futuristic, exciting to look at and have more features than a top of the line Lexus. However, they are usually concept only. The concept car itself seldom goes into production. But many of the features of a concept car will eventually be added to the manufacturer's regular production cars.

After building a concept car, the next step is to build a prototype which is a car that is expected to go into production, albeit with a number of modifications before it finally finds its way to the showroom. The prototype is tested in all kinds of ways, from drive-ability, to performance, to customer reaction and more. With each test, modifications are made – or at least noted - until the prototype is ready for production.

Finally, the production car is made and sold to people like you and me.

This great system probably explains why over the past 30 years, cars have gained so many more innovative features than have refrigerators. Refrigerators and other products normally skip the concept stage and development begins at the prototype stage. Prototypes are tested and a product is developed.

Unfortunately, since the prototype is expected more or less to resemble the final product, prototypes are not usually that innovative. Even if there are numerous brainstorming sessions prior to building the prototype, the most radical ideas are usually disposed of before the prototype is built, with excuses like: "Our customers don't need that"; "It would add too much to the final cost"; "Our competitors don't do that, why should we?" and so on.

In fact, concept vehicles are excellent tools for trying out radical new ideas. Concept vehicles permit vast creative freedom at the design stage, allow you to see how innovative new features will work and let you gauge customer reaction to those features. In addition, concept vehicles can generate a lot of "excitement", which translates into positive publicity.

As a result, the concept product is a tool that should be in every Innovation Master's tool kit. It can be used in product design, service design (through the use of role-plays to demonstrate concept services), marketing approaches and more. Concept products are fun to develop, push people to think creatively and can generate outstanding ideas that have the potential to become product and service innovations.

Indeed, it's a great concept, if you will pardon the pun!

Lesson

The Creative Idea Implementation Plan

There are a number of reasons why creative ideas fail to become innovations. Sometimes it is because the idea, which seems brilliant in concept, is flawed in application. More often, the problem is that organisations invest in creative ideation initiatives (often called "innovation initiatives"), such as brainstorming events, idea management, ideas campaigns and the like, but fail to invest in implementing the most creative ideas that come from those initiatives.

Every Innovation Master has experienced this typical scenario: your company invests in generating ideas via brainstorming events that involve a lot of highly paid managers and researchers. A number of promising creative ideas are generated. Sometimes business plans are developed. Sometimes prototypes are built. Sometimes not. But, at some point between the identification of a promising idea and beginning to implement that idea, the idea is killed. Indeed, this is a problem that plagued Supertrade in its transition from being an innovative start-up in the 60s to its becoming a bureaucratic giant a couple of decades later.

There are many reasons why creative ideas are killed and almost all of them have to do with risk. Implementing a new idea is perceived as risky and people in the company do not wish to undertake that risk. So, the idea is killed. Needless-to-say, investing in a creative idea generation initiative in order to generate creative ideas you will never implement is an expensive method of accomplishing absolutely nothing.

Unwillingness to implement creative ideas is not only a weakness with companies, individuals have the same problem. Imagine a young person applying for a job with Levi Strauss & Co and having the idea to write her CV (résumé in US English) on a pair of Levis jeans and sending it to her perspective employer. Such a creative approach to applying for a job would almost certainly stand out and grab the attention of the hiring person. It could very well result in an interview – particularly if the company values creativity as Levi Strauss does. Or it could result in the CV imprinted jeans being promptly rubbished as ridiculous (note: I have no idea how Levi Strauss would react in this scenario). In my experience, most people who had such a creative idea would be unwilling to risk carrying it out.

Such a waste of creative time, energy and money does no one any good and makes the world a more boring place than it could be.

In order to help individuals and organisations more rationally plan the implementation of creative ideas, I have looked at why ideas are not implemented (at the organisational level and individual level) and have drawn up a Creative Idea Implementation Plan (CIIP). You can even download a Creative Idea Implementation Plan template and accompanying cash-flow template (see link at the end of the article).

The Idea

Before you implement your idea, you need to describe it in detail. Separately, you should describe what makes the idea special, that is: what is the unique selling point (USP)? Once you have done this, ask yourself how you might push the USP even further in order to make your idea even more special.

Benefits and Risks

The next step is to do a simple risk versus benefits analysis. That may sound complex, but might simply be a matter of drawing up a table with a column labelled "benefits" and one called "risks". Then simply list the benefits and risks in their appropriate columns. If the risks are greater than the benefits, you need to rethink your idea and focus on greater benefits. Review your USP in particular.

Stumbling Blocks

A stumbling block is something that can stop, damage or destroy your implementation before it is complete. Early stumbling blocks, such as getting approval from a notoriously conservative committee, lack of budget or risk-adverse managers can kill a creative idea at an early stage of its implementation. To prevent this from happening, you should list all of the possible stumbling blocks that exist between now and the successful implementation of your idea. Then look at each stumbling block and indicate how you will deal with it. Being prepared for stumbling blocks not only makes it easier to get past them, but also impresses the people who are responsible for the stumbling blocks (and most stumbling blocks are caused by people!).

People

Speaking of people, make a list of people – as well as organisations and groups – who should be involved in your implementation. These may be colleagues who will buy into your idea, making it easier to sell to top management or they may be designers who will build a prototype to demonstrate your idea. A complex business idea often requires the involvement of numerous people.

Authorisations

Implementing the idea may include the necessity of gaining authorisations from one or more bodies. Authorisations may include approval from people in your company, licenses from government offices and certificates from professional bodies. If an idea is in a new area, it is best to research relevant government regulations – you may be in for a surprise. For example, here in Belgium, licenses and regulations that apply to a restaurant depend on whether or not it serves potatoes!

Money
Calculate the costs of implementing your idea and what is the likely income. For most business ideas, you will probably want to prepare a cash-flow table to calculate the costs and income over time (you can download our template, see end of article). If you can demonstrate a cash-flow with minimal outlay and a large reward potential, you will find it significantly easier to convince people to buy into your idea.

Milestones
With all but the simplest ideas, you should draw up a list of milestones that must be achieved along the way towards implementing your idea. For example, a new product idea might require a business case, a prototype, market research, product testing, etc. In addition, milestones can be good points for determining whether or not to continue with an idea; or for considering modifications to the idea.

Escape Plan
Very often, when considering implementing a creative idea, committees will water down the idea and make it less risky. Unfortunately, removing risk from an idea is the same as removing creativity. A creative idea with its risk removed is often a mediocre idea. A better approach is to go ahead with a risky, creative idea, but to have an escape plan. For example: if the idea does not meet certain milestones within a determined time frame, you agree to stop it. If sales do not reach a specific target after one year, you stop it. And so on. Predetermining an escape plan mitigates risk and ensures you or your company will not

continue to throw money at an idea that eventually proves unlikely to meet its potential.

Communication Plan

A communication plan clarifies who should learn about the implementation, when they should learn about it and how. A communication plan may also indicate who should not know about the idea implementation, particularly at the early stages. For instance, if you are working on a breakthrough idea, you may want to keep it secret as long as possible to prevent your competitors from learning what you are doing. On the other hand, you might want to communicate about your highly innovative idea immediately in order to be recognised as the first moving innovator behind the new idea.

Even if you are implementing a personal idea, communicating it can help give you the confidence to see it through to completion. Moreover, discussing the idea with friends, family and colleagues may provide valuable input about how to make the idea more innovative.

Action Plan

The last step of the implementation plan is the step-by-step action plan. This will describe every step you take, how long each step will take and what should be achieved. It will incorporate much of the information above. Indeed, by compiling the information above first, you can better develop a cast iron action plan that increases the likeliness that your idea will be implemented effectively. And that is what turns a creative idea into an innovation.

Creative Idea Implementation Plan Template

The Creative Idea Implementation Plan (CIIP) is a template for implementing a creative idea so that it may become a true innovation. CIIP is based on experience in numerous companies around the world and, in particular, is designed to overcome issues that often prevent creative ideas from being brought to fruition. Simply answer these questions. You can download a copy of this template from
http://www.jpb.com/creative/ciip.php

Tasks for you

1. Explain the idea

2. What is unique or special about this idea?

3. How might you push the unique/special elements of the idea (see question above) further?

4. What are the benefits and risks of this idea? Create a chart like this.

Benefits	Risks

5. What issues – or "stumbling blocks" – can you anticipate that might make it difficult or impossible to implement your idea?

6. What actions might you take, for each stumbling block listed above, in order to prevent that stumbling block from killing your idea?

7. Which people, groups or organisations (if any) should you bring into this implementation in order to facilitate its successful implementation?

8. What authorisations must you obtain (if any) to implement this idea? Include any legal licenses or certificates that might be needed.

9. What are the anticipated cost and income potential of this idea? Attach a cash-flow spreadsheet if appropriate. (Note: you may download a cash-flow spreadsheet from http://www.jpb.com/creative/ciip.php – scroll to bottom of page)

10. What milestones should there be in the development of this idea?

11. In the event the implementation does not go to plan, what is your escape plan?

12. Communication plan. Whom, aside from the idea development team, will you tell about this idea and how?

13. Provide a detailed action plan for the implementation of your idea. Include timing information.

14. Additional remarks.

15. Your name, contact information and other relevant data.

Phase 6

Culture

Journey

A Clear Path Ahead

The lift slowly ascended the side of the mountain, offering splendid views down the mountain and allowing us to see how much distance we had covered over the past few hours. The air had taken on a refreshing crispness with the altitude, but it was still pleasant. In the background, we could hear the clanging of the lift machinery somewhat hidden behind the never-ending rustle of the wind.

Eventually the machine slowed to a stop at an iron platform jutting out from the cliff-edge. An elaborate iron lattice fence surrounded the platform. Beyond the platform a partially ruined, yet still elegant Buddhist temple could be seen glimmering in the late afternoon sun.

An elderly Chinese monk in the traditional saffron robe approached us. He had a smile on his face and a glimmer in his eye. "You've made it! I am so glad!"

Jane and I both thanked him.

"Did you know we were coming?" asked Jane.

The monk smiled gently. "I heard the lift start up and I knew someone was coming. Not many people make it here to the temple. And since Mr. Jeffrey is with you, I expect you will be going on to the Temple of Ideas."

"That's right," said Jane.

"The important thing is you made it this far up the mountain and you only have a short distance further to go before you arrive," continued the monk.

"Oh good," said Jane.

"How was your climb? I expect a couple of healthy young people like you are having no trouble with your journey," said the monk.

"Oh, we've run into a few challenges along the way," I said. "For instance, you know that stretch of path to the East of the lift?"

The monk thought for a moment. "You mean near Rang Bun Dal Jai Valley?"

"Yes, that's right. The path has gone to hell and the bridge over the valley is falling apart," I said. "We originally intended to go along the footpath to the Temple of Ideas."

"Oh dear," replied the monk. "That's no good. But surely this way is more convenient, isn't it?"

"Is it?" asked Jane.

"I think so," said the monk looking at me suspiciously. I smiled back at him and I believe he understood that Jane had to make the decisions about the route.

"The map isn't clear about how to get from this temple to our temple," Jane explained.

"Oh, that's very easy, I'll show you. Just follow me," said the monk spinning around. As he did so, a golden amulet fell from his robe. Jane bent over to pick it up and was about to hand it to the monk, when I gently took it from her and handed it to the monk myself. Jane looked at me oddly.

The monk laughed. "Don't worry, young lady. Mr. Jeffrey is not being rude. He just understands our culture. You see, according to our rules, it is prohibited for a Vinaya Buddhist monk to touch a woman."

"Why is that?" asked Jane.

"You are very curious," said the monk with a laugh. "That is wonderful. You will do well in your temple, I am sure. As to your question, it is believed that a monk may be overwhelmed by lust if he is touched by a woman."

"Oh, I see," said Jane thinking.

"I've been a monk so long, I am not sure I would recognise lust even if I were overwhelmed by it," said the monk. "But rules are rules and culture is culture."

"Well, of course, I can respect that," said Jane.

"Good," said the monk. "Now, come this way."

We followed him to the temple. "Would you like to take a peek inside?" he asked.

"Yes, please," said Jane.

"Then you..." began the monk.

"I know. We need to remove our shoes. I know that bit of your culture anyway," said Jane with a smile.

I was pleased to look inside as well. I've been to the Buddhist temple several times, and have always enjoyed looking inside. This temple had obviously been neglected for years, so it had an aged elegance that you seldom see in the Buddhist temples elsewhere in this region.

Inside the temple was a beautiful, yet faded marble floor. Against the far wall was a large, stone Buddha seated. His right hand was held close to his chest, palm outward with his thumb and index finder making a circle. His face displayed Buddha's usual serenity.

"The Buddha is actually carved into the mountain rock," I explained quietly to Jane. "And the temple was built around the statue."

"I see. And is there any meaning to his stance?" asked Jane.

"It is the Vitarka Mudra gesture," explained the monk. It symbolises teaching.

"That's appropriate," said Jane. "I have learned more on this mountain hike than I believe I ever have in a previous hike."

"Oh good," said the monk.

"Excellent, indeed," I agreed.

We went back outside, shod our feet and walked around the temple. On our way, we saw a family laying garlands around a smaller Buddha stature.

"They are making a wish," explained the monk. "Doubtless, they are praying to Buddha that if the wish comes true, they will make a donation to the temple or at least a good cause."

"But I thought Buddha was not a god, just a philosopher.."

"That is true, young lady"

"Jane"

"That is true, Ms. Jane. I don't exactly approve myself. But it is their belief. And I believe that if they believe hard enough, they might make their own wishes come true."

"But then they are crediting Buddha for their own initiative," said Jane.

"Some people find it easier to believe in a higher power than in themselves," observed the monk. "And how about you, Ms. Jane. Do you believe in your ability to achieve what it is you seek?"

Jane thought about this for a moment. "Yes."

"Good. I believe so too," said the monk pointing down a long, clear path framed by trees. "You could not have come this far without belief and you've only to follow that road around the mountain to your destination."

"Is that all?" asked Jane, somewhat surprised.

"Yes," said the monk.

And with that, Jane and I walked up the clear path. As we passed a clearing, we heard a helicopter flying overhead, towards the Temple of Ideas.

Dialogue

A Much Shorter Journey

We zoom in on the helicopter Jane and I just saw, through the cockpit window and inside to see that it is being flown by Alpha, with Beta by his side. They scan the Buddhist temple, glance at Jane and I and then look at each other. They are wearing headsets in order to be able to speak in the noisy cockpit.

Alpha: Oops, no. That's not the temple of ideas, is it?

Beta: I must say, I am amazed at how quickly you worked out where the temple is located. Most people spend months on it.

Alpha: I told you that my secretary was good at that kind of thing. I put her on it full-time and got another secretary to tide me over. Wasn't as good as Helene, but I managed.

Beta: Good for you. But maybe Helene should be here instead of you.

Alpha: Don't be silly, she can't fly a helicopter.

Beta: That's not quite what I meant...

Alpha: Actually, I did invite her to come along, but she thought it would be inappropriate. Probably would be. Anyway, she's jolly good. I'll try and find a more challenging position for

	her. I'll miss her, of course, but she could be doing a lot more for the old biz than catering after me.
Beta:	That's probably a sensible thing to do.
Alpha:	I know. Not like me at all. But Helene's a good lass. Want to keep her happy, you know.
Beta:	And your other people?
Alpha:	Good lord, there's thousands of them! How can I keep them happy?
Beta:	Well, my Innovation Master – you'll meet her soon – has been spending a lot of time helping us establish what she calls a "culture of innovation".
Alpha:	A what?
Beta:	A culture of innovation, you know, an environment where people are comfortable about creativity and innovation.
Alpha:	Good lord! You need a special environment to innovate!?
Beta:	Apparently. Otherwise people just don't bother doing anything new – just the same old thing day in and day out. If you want your people to share ideas, try out new concepts and develop innovative projects, it seems you really ought to have a culture of innovation.
Alpha:	Sounds dodgy.
Beta:	Not at all! It's actually created a jolly pleasant working atmosphere all around, with happy employees virtually skip-

ping from the car park to their desks and giggling the day away.

Alpha: Are you sure they are not on drugs? I remember some of the things we did back in the 60s and 70s.

Beta: Good lord, no! No. Perhaps I exaggerate ever so slightly. But, the point is, there is a level of happiness in our offices that I haven't seen before.

Alpha: I'm not sure you want employees too happy. Are they getting things done or just telling jokes and giggling all day long?

Beta: Productivity is up.

Alpha: Well, that's good. Maybe I should look into this culture of innovation thing myself.

Beta: And we are working on a number of new product ideas. A good 20% of our stuff for next year will be brand spanking new!

Alpha: Perhaps it's you who's on drugs...

Beta: Don't be silly old friend.

Alpha: So, you're saying this innovation thing really is the bee's knees.

Beta: No doubt about it!

Alpha: I say, if you don't mind changing the subject a tad, there's the hotel where you first brought up this whole discussion of Innovation and the Temple of Ideas. [Alpha points to a building in the distance]

Beta: Yes, I believe you are right.

Alpha: Of course I am right. In fact, when I mentioned it to Helene, it helped her work out where the Temple was.

Beta: Speaking of the temple, there she is [Beta points to a complex of ancient building straight ahead.]

Alpha: Oh my! That is a stunning-looking hideaway. No wonder you keep sneaking off this way.

Beta: It is beautiful. But they teach good stuff here, too.

Alpha: So I gather.

Can I fly straight in?

Beta: Yes there's a platform around there where you can land this thing.

Alpha: Marvellous. Say, I wonder if that couple we saw at the other Buddhist temple were also coming this way.

Beta: I expect so.

Have we set down? Well, that was a gentle landing. You're good at this.

Alpha: Yes, I do have my skills.

Beta: I know you do, old friend. Otherwise, you wouldn't be here.

Lesson

A Dozen Ingredients for a Culture of Innovation

As Beta explained to Alpha, a culture of innovation is critical if you really want your company to be an innovator. Unfortunately, much business practice today tends to go against such a culture, hence you will probably need to make some changes in the way people work in your offices.

The good news is, the changes are for the better. A culture of innovation also creates a very pleasant working environment where people feel more comfortable about taking risk and trying new things. Moreover, most people take pride in working for a known innovative leader (think about Apple, Google, etc.).

Let's take a look at exactly what a culture of innovation is and what you need to do to establish one.

Definition of a Culture of Innovation
A culture of innovation is very simply a workplace environment that constantly encourages people to think creatively and facilitates implementing creative ideas so that they may become innovations. It is important to note that our definition includes the terms "creativity" and "innovation". That is because innovative solutions are the result of implemented creative ideas.

Since humans are creative thinkers and groups comprise humans, a culture of innovation needs to motivate the groups and individuals to think creatively. At the same time, if the most viable of those creative ideas are not implemented, the company might be considered creative, but it would not be an innovative firm. Thus to achieve a culture of innovation you need both creativity and innovation.

Ingredients

Let us look at the 12 basic ingredients necessary for a culture of innovation.

1. Top Management Buy-In

A culture of innovation has to start at the very top of an organisation. If top management do not embrace innovation, they can hardly expect their employees to do so either.

2. Trust

Several surveys into innovation, including one by PWC earlier this millennium[1], cite trust as being one of the most crucial ingredients to a culture of innovation. This is not surprising. Being creative, particularly in a corporate environment, is risky. Sharing a creative idea with your colleagues might well result in your being ridiculed. Worse, if the idea conflicts with the pet project of another employee, especially if she is your senior, it could easily get you in trouble. Even in firms that value creative ideas, there is the danger that a manager might steal your idea and present it to top management as her own in order to get credit for the idea.

However, if people trust top management, their colleagues and the firm itself, they can be more comfortable about sharing ideas without fear of unpleasant consequences.

3. Priority of Innovation (Often Confused with Time)

Several surveys I have seen, including one I published in Report 103[2], have indicated that lack of time is a major hurdle to innovation. But a moment's thought suggests that this is nonsense. Every full time employee in Europe works at least a 35-hour week. Most work more. Americans and Japanese tend to work much more. Clearly people who say that they do not have time to innovate are wrong. They have time. But, in their firms, innovation is of a very low priority. They give priority to other tasks ahead of creative problem solving, creative thinking, experimentation and the implementation of innovative ideas.

But bear in mind that employees in very innovative firms do not have access to a time warp device that gives them more time in a day. No. Their firms simply give innovation a top priority.

If you want a culture of innovation in your firm, creativity and innovation have to take priority over excessive reporting, PowerPoint slide making, long meetings, reading irrelevant e-mails and other tasks that take priority in non-innovative firms. We'll look at this in more detail in the next lesson.

4. Freedom to Take Action

In many firms, especially large bureaucratic ones, taking action on any idea requires following complex procedures, obtaining multiple approvals and often trial by ultra-conservative-thinking committees. Getting an unusual idea (most creative ideas are unusual ideas, otherwise they would have been thought up long ago) past all of these hurdles is nearly impossible. In a culture of innovation, it should be dead easy for employees to take action on creative ideas. Of course safeguards should exist; but not to avoid risk at all cost. Rather to identify when an idea is not working and stopping its implementation so that another creative idea can be tried out.

In a culture of innovation, employees should constantly be experimenting with new ideas and reporting on results whether negative or positive.

5. Freedom to Make Mistakes
Of course if employees have the freedom to take action (as described in point 4), they will make mistakes. In many firms, mistakes lead to consequences ranging from reprimand to dismissal. In a culture of innovation, on the other hand, employees must have the freedom to make mistakes, the opportunity to learn from them and the means to share what they have learned without fear of consequences.

6. Reward Rather than Stifle Creative Thinking
If an employee shares with you a crazy idea that you know top management would never approve and for which you could not possibly get the budget, how do you react? Most people, of course, would immediately say to the employee: "That's crazy! Management would never approve an idea like that and we don't have the budget anyway." But such a response is highly detrimental to creative thinking. It tells the idea-sharer that you won't even consider highly creative ideas.

A much better response would be to pause for a moment, think about the idea and reply: "That's brilliant! I love the fact that you are thinking creatively. But you know management will have some problems with your idea, not least of which will be budget. How might we convince management to give it a try?"

This time, you have verbally rewarded the idea sharer with a complement and by giving her a creative challenge to improve her idea even further. That shows respect for her thinking.

In a culture of innovation, creative ideas are always recognised and rewarded and creative thinkers are challenged to improve their ideas so that they are more likely to become profitable innovations.

7. Collaboration Tools

A key to organisational innovation is collaboration. Great ideas are seldom the exclusive work of a lonely, but brilliant scientist toiling away in the laboratory. Rather they are the result of collaborative development of ideas by multiple individuals and teams. Implementing those ideas requires further collaboration, bringing in people to help in the various stages of developing the idea.

In small innovative companies, collaboration is easy. People simply meet up in various corners to share ideas. They e-mail and telephone each other and discuss their thoughts over lunch. But, once a firm has 100 or more employees, collaborative tools such as innovation process management applications, wikis, on-line conferencing applications, document sharing facilities and other tools foster collaboration. Particularly important is to encourage the development of diverse teams of people from different locations, divisions and backgrounds. In large organisations, people tend to know their closest colleagues – usually others in their divisions – best. This makes it harder to develop collaborative relationships with people in remote locations and completely different divisions. Tools to help find expertise and encourage networking across the enterprise as well as outside the enterprise can help tremendously.

8. Places and Opportunities to Talk

In order to collaborate, people do not only need collaboration tools. They need places they can meet up and talk. Ideally, you should have lots of places in your firm where people can sit down and share ideas. These should range from large conference rooms, for structured meetings, to small clusters of chairs around tables where people can simply meet and talk. In a culture of innovation, creative collaboration is a daily activity.

9. Places and Opportunities to Work in Isolation

While collaboration is critical for innovative thinking, people also sometimes need to be able to work in isolation, undistracted by colleagues. They may need quiet or the opportunity simply to sit and think without fear that they will look like zombies. In open plan offices where people face each other and work in crowds all day long, employees do not have the opportunity for quiet thought and meditation. If your office is an open plan one, be sure there are not only places for people to meet up, but also places for people to go in order to be alone!

10. Access to Information

In order to develop and analyse creative ideas, people need access to information. Fortunately, Google makes it easier than ever to find data. But information does not come only from web pages. Being able to call contacts in other firms, participate in web forums, go to professional events and even visit the library is important in the development of ideas.

11. Transparency

Employees should also be able to access internal information of all kinds. Thus, in a culture of innovation, the organisation should operate with maximum transparency, sharing not only ideas, but information on the evaluation and implementation of those ideas. Management should keep employees informed of new strategies, anticipated change and more. The more employees know and understand about the operations of their firm, the better they are able to help the firm innovate. Moreover, transparency leads to trust. And we have already learned about how important that is to a culture of innovation!

12. Humour

Humour and creativity go hand in hand, particularly in the business world. In the most innovative companies, you will regularly hear people laughing. Employees share jokes and appreciate jokes. There are two reasons for this. Firstly, humour is very similar to creativity. It is about bringing together disparate concepts in unusual ways – ways that are funny in the case of humour. Secondly, if people are in a comfortable, trusting environment, they are more likely to relax and laugh. And this is important for creativity too. When people relax and joke about ideas, they become increasingly likely to come up with really crazy ideas. And every now and again, one of those really crazy ideas becomes the basis for a breakthrough innovation.

Conclusion

There you have it. A dozen basic ingredients for a culture of innovation. Unfortunately, you cannot create a culture of innovation overnight. It takes time to build up trust, introduce new tools and processes, and implement change in the way people work. But if innovation truly is important to your firm, you need to begin working on establishing a culture of innovation now.

On a positive note, this lesson could also have been entitled "A Dozen Descriptors of a Really Great Place to Work!" That's because a culture of innovation empowers creative thinkers, enables them to take pride in their work and allows them to enjoy what they are doing.

References

1. **PriceWaterhouseCoopers Innovation Survey** (2002)
2. Wayne Morris (2005) "A Survey of Organisational Creativity" (Paper) **JPB.COM** http://www.jpb.com/creative/OrganisationalCreativityMoris.pdf

Lesson

Prioritising Innovation

As Alpha and Beta noted in one of their dialogues, it is not enough to say that Innovation is your number one priority. Lots of companies can and do say just that. You actually have to turn innovation into your number one priority. This is critical to a culture of innovation as well as to your business's innovation process itself.

But where does innovation sit on the priority list of your employees? Probably further down that list than you would like. In my experience, in most organisations, people will treat innovation as an optional action to be considered only when they have completed the mundane tasks of filling in spreadsheets, attending too many meetings and reading through the endless cc's of emails they receive daily.

Why is this? Let's find out!

Time to Innovate
A couple of years ago, jpb.com published a research report titled: "A Survey of Organisational Creativity", by Wayne Morris. It found that the number one barrier to organisational creativity, and hence innovation, is lack of time. In the report, Wayne wrote: "More respondents raised the issue of time as the most important factor in enhancing organisational creativity than any other with comments such as, "'Just having uninterrupted time would do it for me. It's so rare that I make space and time in my day to just think. I know that when I do it works really well for me and I get a lot more satisfaction from my work. It re-

mains a real challenge for me."'[1] Other research I have seen has had similar findings.

But the truth is, employees have lots of time. In the developed world, most organisations stipulate a 35-40 hour work week. Employees in the USA and Japan are notorious for exceeding the standard working week. Seven or eight or more hours a day is, in fact, a lot of time to be creative.

It's Not Time, It's Priorities

So, the problem is clearly not that employees do not have sufficient time to be creative. Rather, they believe that being creative is of such little importance, that every other task in their job description should be done first. Thus, even though management might be shouting that "Innovation is our number one priority", most employees feel that "Putting the financial projections for the third quarter into a nifty spreadsheet in time for tomorrow's division meeting is my number one priority" and innovation probably comes in at around priority number 50, after answering unimportant e-mails, tidying the desk and filing away those reports from marketing.

Why Innovation Is a Low Priority for Many

There are several reasons for this. First and foremost, although management is shouting that "Innovation is the company's number one priority", it is not really communicating to employees that innovation is their number one priority. (Quick definition: corporate innovation = the profitable implementation of creative ideas). Until that is communicated to employees, few will bother with active creative thinking.

This brings us to our second reason. Being creative often does not look like work. My creative juices flow best when I walk. This helps me not only come up with ideas, but it also helps me analyse ideas and make decisions. Others sit in chairs and stare out the window. Some people are best in the bathtub. Unfortunately, none of these activities looks like real work.

If substantial parts of your offices are cubical farms or open plan desks, employees are going to be self-conscious about sitting and thinking. They know it will not look like they are working and they will fear being looked down upon by their neighbouring colleagues.

The third reason is that creativity and innovation are very fuzzy concepts. While most employees are very clear on what is involved in preparing a financial projection, how to respond to a customer query and what information to include in a report, few know just what is involved in being creative and innovative. Thus, for them it is easier to be busy with concrete tasks with clear rules rather than to have to struggle with vague notions of being creative.

Of course, employees generally receive some kind of training on how to complete a financial projection spreadsheet, the company style for internal reports and how to respond to customer queries. Few receive training on how to be creative.

What You Can Do

There are several things you can do to ensure that your employees prioritise innovation.

1. **Practice what you preach**. Demonstrate that you are spending time working on creative ideas, developing innovative projects and just thinking. Thinking is an important element to innovation. Yet many employees will be reluctant to sit and think for fear it looks like they are not doing anything. Would you rather your knowledge workers perform active yet mindless tasks or quiet, mindful tasks?

2. **Training.** Provide your employees with training on how to think more creatively and, probably even more importantly, how they can apply creative thinking to their work.

3. **Rewards.** A rewards system (see the first lesson on Innovation Planning) can go far towards encouraging people to think more creatively – not only because they want to receive rewards, but also because the rewards legitimise creativity as an important activity for the company.

4. **Actions.** Ideas campaigns, brainstorming events or other initiatives based around innovation challenges help employees focus their creative thinking. This has the added benefits of focusing creativity on your business needs and putting employees in a "problem solving" state of mind rather than the somewhat fuzzier "being creative" state of mind.

Once it is clear that innovation really is your company's top priority – and not just a slogan – you will find that people start having much more time to participate in innovation. But remember, innovation is not just about ideas. It is also about breaking down problems, evaluating ideas, developing ideas and implementing them.

The quiet financial analyst who never seems to have ideas, but can prepare impressive financial projections of new project ideas is as much a part of the innovation process as the creative guy who has lots of clever ideas.

Reference

1. Wayne Morris (2005) "A Survey of Organisational Creativity" (Paper) **JPB.COM**
http://www.jpb.com/creative/OrganisationalCreativityMorris.pdf

Lesson

Downsizing the Workforce Downsizes Innovation

When Supertrade ran into financial difficulties as a result of the economic slowdown exacerbated by the mismanagement of Jack III, they had on a couple of occasions to lay off staff in order to keep payroll costs down. As a result, their already weak innovation performance became even weaker. This is not surprising. Research shows that downsizing is bad for innovation for two key reasons: broken strategic links and broken trust. Let's see why this is so.

Strategic Linking

As you know, business innovation – and especially new product innovation – is almost never the result of one creative genius who sits in a laboratory inventing things. Rather, innovations are developed from the first germ of an idea, through to a developed concept and eventual product, service or process via collaboration.

Colleagues in an organisation share ideas on how to solve problems. As good ideas are identified, they are built upon in conversations, team meetings, e-mail exchanges and by using collaborative tools. Creative people seek feedback on ideas from their more analytical colleagues. Marketing people might be asked to review product ideas. Research people build and test prototypes and so on.

According to research by Dougherty and Bowman[1], new product innovation relies on "strategic linking". People need to link not only to other innovators, but to managers who can champion their ideas, sales people who can sell the resulting products and others. Keith Sawyer uses the term "collaborative web"[2] to describe this network of links. When collaborative webs break down owing to lay-offs, employees have to start all over in building up a new collaborative web.

In their study of a dozen firms, Dougherty and Bowman found a direct correlation with the extent of a firm's downsizing and the inability of people to solve strategic linking problems. The firms with the least downsizing solved 48% of strategic linking problems; the ones with the most solved only 23%.

They found that in most firms in which large numbers of employees were dismissed, management paid almost no attention to product innovation. Their advice: "To overcome the negative consequences of downsizing on product innovation, managers should support innovation sponsors and champions, and retain "old timers" who constitute the network. They should also bolster the network by building more connections among departments, and between new and established businesses. Finally, they should incorporate innovation directly into their firm's strategy. "

I would add that management also needs to help employees build new collaborative webs. This can be done through internal networking activities; building the equivalent of marketplaces where employees can learn about other divisions and how to work with them; and bringing diverse people into meetings. Activities such as these bring people into contact with colleagues they might otherwise never meet and thus facilitates building new collaborative webs.

Unfortunately, these activities, while having substantial long term pay-off, are unlikely to be seen as productive in the short term. Employees themselves will be reluctant to do anything that might be perceived as non-productive and middle managers will be equally unenthusiastic about sponsoring such activities. Thus senior managers must make clear the long term benefits of networking to build new collaborative webs.

Indeed, as a senior manager, it is absolutely critical that you minimise disruption of the creative web, provide methods for rebuilding webs and stress the value of those webs as well as the importance of time spent on networking. Your company's innovativeness depends on it!

Broken Trust

Research on innovative companies often demonstrates that trust is a critical ingredient. If employees trust each other, trust their managers and trust their brand, they are more than willing to risk being creative and building ideas that can turn into innovations. They do not fear that they will be reprimanded if an idea does not pan out. They are not worried about managers stealing credit for their ideas and they know they will not be laughed at for making an outrageous suggestion.

Unfortunately, lay-offs have an unpleasant tendency to destroy trust. Employees are no longer sure if they have a future in their company. They begin to worry that time devoted to developing a creative idea might be perceived as time wasted. They worry that if they do not demonstrate productivity, they will be in the next batch of dismissed colleagues. They worry that more desperate colleagues might steal their ideas. And that all kills trust.

And once this trust dies, people spend less time trying to be more innovative. They keep ideas to themselves and avoid rocking the boat. And that is not good for innovation.

Again, it is up to management to stress the increased importance of innovation to the firm and encourage time spent on innovative projects. Indeed, management should explicitly state that time spent on innovative projects is considered productive time.

It is also important to bear in mind that if the focus of your company's innovation strategy is going to change, this should also be communicated to employees. It is understandable that management may want to focus innovation on quick-to-market ideas rather than long term projects that might not pay off in five years. If so, employees need to understand this new focus so they can support it.

The Best Solution
Of course, the best thing you can do for the innovative future of your firm is not to downsize. But when you have no other option, then it is critical to keep innovation in mind when planning your downsizing.

References:
1. Deborah Dougherty and Edward H. Bowman (1995) "The effects of organizational downsizing on product innovation." California Management Review, Vol. 37 No. 4, Summer issue
2. Kieth Sawyer, "The Downside of Downsizing" (2008) **Creativity and Innovation** (Blog) http://keithsawyer.wordpress.com/2008/11/14/the-downside-of-downsizing/

Lesson

Glorious Mistakes

In Supertrade's early days, its entrepreneurial founders were making mistakes left and right. They usually laughed about these over a beer at the end of the day. And in laughing, they often came up with solutions – often only half seriously. However, by the next day, some of these ideas actually seemed promising. Fortunately, the trio had made it a habit to jot down all their ideas on beer mats which were brought to the office the next day.

However, as the company grew and became more bureaucratic, mistakes were less welcome. During the management of Jack III, senior management were afraid to make mistakes. And this fear trickled down the firm creating a highly risk-adverse culture. Not surprisingly, this was not at all good for their innovation process!

We Do Not Let Our Children Learn from Mistakes!
It is a cliché to say that we learn from our mistakes. Indeed, we tend to say it more than we practice it. Indeed, in most cultures, young children are taught by memorising correct answers and being marked down for mistakes.

From their early school days, most children are given correct answers to basic questions, such as maths equations, spelling, grammar and the like. Then they are taught to memorise these answers by repeating them over and over again until the question and answer pairs are embedded in their young brains and those children can say six times six is 36 without even thinking about it. The assumption is that if a child were at some point to start giving an incorrect answer – such as six times six is 38 – the wrong answer would embed itself in her mind and she would have to work doubly hard to unlearn the wrong answer and then learn the correct answer. Hence the emphasis on memorising correct responses to such questions.

It's compelling logic. But it is wrong. Research[1,2] has shown the opposite to be true. Children actually learn better when they are put in situations that increase the likelihood that they will make errors. A number of experiments were designed to test this assumption. In each of these experiments, children were given information to learn. In one group, the children were given tasks in which they first had to attempt to retrieve on their own answers to difficult questions. In this group, most of the children did indeed get their initial answers wrong. Then, they were given the correct answers to the questions. It was found that the children in this group learned the information better than the children the group that was taught the information using the old-fashioned rote-learning method.

Don't Reach for Google

As an adult, there is a lesson to be learned here. If you believe you do not know the answer to a challenging problem, do not immediately Google the problem. Instead, attempt to work out the answer using your own knowledge, experience and assumptions. Then Google. By so doing, you are more likely to learn the correct solution to the problem. Moreover, the process of correcting yourself is likely to be enlightening as well. Why was your guess wrong? What assumptions did you make in the process of making your guess? Alternatively, you may discover that your solution is more effective than what you have found on Google. That's even better!

As a manager, the lesson to be learned is not to tell starter employees precisely how to do their tasks. Rather, you should let them attempt to work out for themselves how to solve problems – and then, if they fail, give them instructions. This has a twofold benefit. Firstly, new employees will learn how to perform tasks better this way. Secondly, in attempting to come up with their own approach to solving tasks, they may actually come up with a better approach than your company is currently using. That is the first step in the path to innovation! It goes without saying that when employees might harm themselves or others, this is not the best approach to take – unless of course you are using simulations or another method to prevent injury.

At a higher level of business, there often are not defined means of accomplishing tasks. Indeed, it is at this level that you want employees to demonstrate creative thinking in order to solve problems. Fortunately, if you have allowed starter employees to learn by making mistakes, experienced employees are likely to be both more knowledgeable and more creative in their thinking. This can only work to your company's advantage!

Mistakes: an Alternative to Training

There is a story, most likely apocryphal, of a manager who launches a major project only to see it fail spectacularly. Rather than revolutionising the business, his company loses $20 million. The manager sends his letter of resignation to the CEO and is in his office gathering his things when his secretary tells the manager that the CEO would like to see him right now.

The manager goes into the CEO's office and immediately launches into an apology: "I know I blew it with that project. I've sent you my letter of resignation. I am sorry."

The CEO takes the letter of resignation, tears into pieces and says, "Son, that $20 million was the most expensive on-the-job training in the history of this company. If you think I am going to let you leave after all you have learned, you must be out of your mind."

And the truth is, we do learn from mistakes. I learned a great deal about organisational innovation by spending a number of years working in organisations that did everything they could to hinder innovation. By seeing what did not work, I was able to visualise models and behaviours that I believed would work better. Then, first by looking at successful innovators as well as social-psychological research, I was able to confirm some of my theories (and abandon others). Later, in my current work, I have been able to put these models to the test.

Simply looking at successful innovators would not have been enough to allow me to fully understand what works and what does not work in terms of organisational innovation. Looking at failed innovators taught me much more.

Not Admitting Mistakes Is More Costly

In organisations where mistakes are considered unacceptable, employees are understandably reluctant to admit it when things go wrong. As a result, when a project is failing, the employee in charge is often inclined to continue the project, rather than admit failure. This can be an expensive waste of resources. A hopeless project killed early will cost the company far less than a hopeless project that is allowed to eat resources for months in hopes a miracle will occur. Clearly, even in companies where mistakes are unwelcome, this is not a desirable approach!

This scenario demonstrates two problems with respect to the fear of mistakes. One is the reluctance of people to admit to a mistake, even when it is clear things are going wrong. The second is a reluctance to ask for help to solve a problem, out of fear that asking for help will flag the mistake. Hence, not only are employees reluctant to admit that a project is failing, they are equally reluctant to ask for help that could prevent, or even reverse a failure!

That is a shame. Not only is there much to learn from mistakes. They can also spark off breakthrough innovations.

Some Mistakes Lead to Great Inventions

Perhaps the most famous story of a great invention being discovered as a result of an accident or mistake is the discovery of Penicillin by Alexander Fleming[3]. He had been studying staphylococci, a kind of bacteria that can often cause illness in humans. Just before leaving on holiday, he stacked a number of cultures of staphylococci on his lab table and left them there (apparently, he was notoriously untidy). Upon his return, he observed that one culture was contaminated with a fungus, and that the colonies of staphylococci that had immediately surrounded it had been destroyed, while the colonies further away were normal. The fungus was identified as being of the Penicillium genus and hence the name of the first antibiotic and arguably one of the most important discoveries in medical history.

There are two "what-ifs" to consider here. Firstly, what if Mr. Fleming was working in a large company in which mistakes were not tolerated? Upon returning from holiday and seeing that his lab was a mess, or that something was not right with some of his cultures, his first reaction might have been promptly to clean and sterilise everything before his superiors discovered his mistake.

Alternatively, what if Mr. Fleming did not have the medical knowledge that he did actually have.? Or what if he simply did not have an inquisitive mind? In either case, he might not have realised the powerful implications hidden in the Petri dish with the fungus.

However, the world is fortunate that Fleming was not employed in a bureaucratic organisation with zero tolerance for mistakes and that he was a brilliant biologist with an inquisitive mind.

What Your Organisation Can Learn from Mistakes

There is no doubt about it, mistakes are proven learning exercises. So much so that managers should sometimes encourage mistakes, especially during the early learning phase of new employees. When people make mistakes, when projects go wrong, when teams screw up, their errors should not be swept under the corporate carpet and forgotten. Rather, they should be shared so that not only the people making the mistakes, but also their colleagues, can learn from those mistakes.

Moreover, you never know. By sharing the events that led up to a mistake and the results, someone in your firm may observe an opportunity to profit. More than one breakthrough innovation has been discovered this way. And many more will be – perhaps some of them will be discovered by you and your colleagues.

References

1. Nate Kornell, Matthew Jensen Hays, Robert A Bjork, (July 2009) "Unsuccessful retrieval attempts enhance subsequent learning." **Journal of Experimental Psychology: Learning, Memory, and Cognition**, Vol 35(4), 989-998.

2. Lindsey Richland, Nate Kornell, Liche Kao (2009)" The Pretesting Effect: Do Unsuccessful Retrieval Attempts Enhance Learning?", **Journal of Experimental Psychology: Applied,** Vol. 15, No. 3, 243–257

3. "Alexander Fleming" (2001-2010) **Wikipedia;** http://en.wikipedia.org/wiki/Alexander_Fleming

Phase 7

Arrival

Dialogue

Arrival

The helicopter has landed in a large platform surrounded by an ancient concrete railing. Beyond is the sky. Alpha and Beta have left the helicopter and walk up to a small building where Judy, the senior Innovation Master and head of the Temple of Ideas, is waiting for them.

Judy:	My, my. You have certainly found your way here awfully quickly.
Alpha:	May I take that as a compliment?
Judy:	You may, but be sure to give it to Helene. I expect she played a role in helping you find us.
Alpha:	She did indeed. She's a clever ducky.
Judy:	She is. Anyway, welcome to the Temple of Ideas, Alpha. Beta, it's good to see you again, as always.
Beta:	Thank you, Judy. A pleasure to see you, too.
Judy:	It's well that you came with him, this is not the easiest place to spot from the sky.
Beta:	May I ask a question?
Judy:	Of course.

Beta: No offence to Alpha…

Alpha: None taken so far, but tread carefully, old friend.

Beta: But, it took me months to work out the location of the Temple and I climbed this mountain to get here. I was welcomed, of course, by you. And my Innovation Master told me that the efforts to find the Temple and climb this mountain were a part of my education and that they demonstrated my commitment to learning to become an Innovation Master.

Judy: Yes, that is all true.

Beta: Yet, my friend here had his secretary locate the Temple and flew in on a helicopter – all in a matter of days. Nevertheless, he is also welcome here.

Judy: [Laughing] I can see your point. Don't be angry, but there are two kinds of creative minds that make suitable Innovation Masters. Some, like you, are willing to work hard in order to learn how to lead an innovation process in your company.

Others, like Alpha here, are simply very lazy achievers. They want to make their lives and work easy and, often subconsciously, use creativity and innovation to achieve that.

Alpha: I'll take that as a compliment

Judy: Please do. People like you actually accomplish a great deal more than others – or you – think.

Alpha: I'll also take that as a compliment. Thank you.

Judy: My pleasure. But that is enough complimenting for the time being. I believe we have a couple of people just arriving via the footpath.

Beta: Aye, I believe we passed them flying here.

Judy: I'll greet them now. Meanwhile, Beta, why don't you take Alpha to the House of Reflection and have them set him up with a room.

Beta: It would be my pleasure.

Judy: And I trust you both will join me and the other newcomers for dinner at eight.

Beta: Absolutely.

Alpha: I'd love to. I've heard wonderful things about your wine cellar [Beta blushes slightly]. I hope I'll have a chance to confirm that.

Judy: We'll see. Goodbye for now.

Alpha: Bye bye.

Beta: See you.

Alpha: She seems like an awfully nice bird.

Beta: She is. Now let's get you settled in and then [looks at his watch], I believe the time would be about right for a drink, don't you?

Alpha: Absolutely, old friend. Absolutely.

Journey

Arrival

We followed the mountain trail in the brisk, cool wind, passing a variety of pine trees that lined the path. The trail worked its way around the top of the mountain, through a few tunnels and before long, we could see the wall around the Temple of Ideas, shimmering in the sunlight. As we came closer, buildings and even people became visible. The Temple is truly a beautiful sight and I never tire of approaching it via this footpath.

"Oh my, it's stunning!" said Jane.

"Isn't it?" I agreed.

We walked through the open gate. On closer inspection, it was clear that the temple was very old. Centuries of weather had worn down the walls and the buildings, giving the place a look of elegant antiquity. We came into the main compound. Before us stood the main building with a grand stairway in front. Coming down the stairs was Judy, the senior Innovation Master and head of the Temple of Ideas. Judy was a woman in late middle age, with a shock of silver hair and a long, flowing gown. Although her face was lined, they were lines that reflected a life of laughter and smiling.

"You must be Jane!" she said, her eyes twinkling with delight which was reflected in her smile.

"Why, yes, I am," said Jane, slightly flabbergasted at being recognised.

"I've heard such good things about you, your work and your mind. I was delighted to learn that you were coming."

"How did you know?" asked Jane, with a tinge of suspicion marring her pleasure at being recognised.

"Why Michael Zimmermann" said Judy. "He and I studied Social Psychology together."

"But he said he didn't know where the Temple of Ideas was located," Jane replied. Seeing that I was looking a touch perplexed, she added, "He's an old professor of mine as well as the guy who told me about the Temple."

"Jeffrey, why don't you take Jane to the House of Reflection and have them set her up with rooms there for her stay. Then you can both relax and, I hope, join me for dinner at eight."

I did as I was told and took Jane to her rooms. From the picture window, we could see a magnificent view down the mountain. "You've come far," I told her. "After this it only gets easier".

Then I left her and went to my own rooms elsewhere in the House. There I put on Bach's Air from Orchestral Suite no. 3, took out my notebook and made notes on the journey. I've been here a while and I often bring people up the mountain. Nevertheless, I always learn something new and I am always inspired by the journey and the vision of the Temple of Ideas at the end of the journey.

Lesson

Departing Thought

Let us leave Jane, Alpha, Beta and me in order to reflect upon the most important person here: you. Let's start with a question.

Who is the most innovative person in your organisation?

That is a trick question, of course. Within the organisational context, innovation is not an individual thing. Rather it is a collaborative act that involves many people working together. If you did name an individual, the chances are that you were actually answering a different question all together, namely: "Who is the most creative thinker in your organisation?" But, as you and I both know, creativity and innovation are very different things. Creativity is an intellectual process of combining two or more existing ideas in order to create a new idea. Innovation (in the corporate world) is the implementation of creative ideas in order to generate value for the organisation, typically through increased income, reduced operational costs or both.

In most organisations even creativity is not the preserve of an individual. Rather it is a collaborative act. Yes, the initial spark of an idea often comes from an individual creative thinker. But it is rare that the original spark is sufficient to be implemented immediately. Rather, people within the firm collaborate to improve upon the idea. That is part of the creative process as well as the innovative process.

A Scenario

Let's imagine a little scenario. You are a high level manager in Supertrade. One evening after work you go out for a glass of wine or a cup of tea (or whatever is your favourite drink for relaxation) with a couple of friendly colleagues from the office. While joking around, you suggest that the company's next big product will be intelligent shopping trolleys that not only keep track of what customers put in them, but which also communicate with other shopping trolleys, the shop's network and even the customer pushing it. As the evening goes on, you and your colleagues' ideas get more elaborate and even preposterous. You have a good laugh, but think there might be something to the ideas. Because you are a good creative thinker, you carry a notebook around with you. So, you write down some notes about intelligent shopping trolleys before going home.

The next day, you may find that each of your colleagues also thinks that she had came up with the intelligent shopping trolley idea. In fact, you all are right. You and your colleagues all contributed elements to the idea. You may have kicked off the original idea that started the conversation. But had the conversation not happened, the idea would not have been developed into the more sophisticated concept that you wrote down in your notebook.

In fact, many creative ideas start off this way, in an open discussion between colleagues. However an idea is nothing more than an idea unless you do something with it.

Developing the Idea

You continue to like the idea of intelligent shopping trolleys. So, the first thing you do is bring together a few colleagues from various divisions in order to explore the idea. People make suggestions on improving it. The marketing manager suggests that the trolleys could capture and broadcast advertising messages from products as it is pushed around a shop. Someone else suggests that the trolleys might be designed to recognise regular customers and point out special offers that would appeal to them.

The idea is getting better and better as more people build upon it. Indeed, you are now taking it seriously and need to draw up a business plan. However, Supertrade lacks internal expertise in the more sophisticated computer technology required for the intelligent shopping trolleys. Hence you tap into your network to find someone with suitable expertise and you give him a call. He puts you in touch with a small firm that specialises in designing complex scanning devices. You discuss your idea with a project manager at the firm and she suggests a few ideas that would make your intelligent shopping trolleys even better.

As you can see, by involving a diverse group of people in the idea development phase, you improve upon the idea considerably. At this stage, the idea has moved from being a simple idea to being a concept that is the sum of many ideas.

Realising the Idea
At this time, you will need to sell your concept to people who can authorise the budget for the launch of a radical new product. Assume that thanks to your charm, a cool prototype and a compelling business case, this step is easy. Now, you need to implement the concept and turn it into an innovation.

In this day and age, you will probably outsource the development of the necessary software to a firm in India or Eastern Europe rather than start a new programming business unit for this one project. Again, you will likely get from your suppliers feedback and suggestions which will add further creativity to the concept.

While this is happening, you also need to work with your people in marketing and sales. After all, no matter how potentially innovative your product may be, if you cannot sell it, it does not do your firm much good. And if prospective customers neither know about nor can find your product in the shops, it will not sell. Getting over these issues is, of course, the job of sales and marketing.

They will also need to be creative in order to help the intelligent shopping trolleys become a commercial success. This will involve advertising, sales promotions, public relations work and more. Each of these steps requires more collaborative creativity in order to succeed.

And the Innovation

After all this collaboration and hard work, let's assume the intelligent shopping trolleys are launched in the market place and become wildly successful. Supertrade doubles its turnover and is featured in Fortune, Wired, Forbes and Shopkeepers' Technology Magazine. There is no doubt about it, the creative idea you and your friends conceived over drinks in the pub has turned into a true innovation.

But who was the innovator?

Why all of you were, of course!

Conclusion

There is one simple lesson to be learned here: true innovation is a collaborative act. There are no individual innovators in your firm.

As a result, if you want to encourage innovation in your firm, your focus should not be on enabling individuals to be more innovative (which does not even make sense). Rather it should be about facilitating innovative networks that allow people to collaborate on developing ideas which allow them to identify experts who can help them to build their ideas into concepts; and providing employees with the freedom to contact outsiders for inspiration and support in turning creative ideas into innovations.

Moreover, if you are rewarding innovators in your firm, be sure to reward all involved. In the example above, if you are the only person who is rewarded, for having the initial idea, particularly if the reward is substantial, there is a good chance that other people in your innovation network will be upset. And this will discourage them from being so cooperative in the future.

Innovation grows in networks and stagnates when trapped in individuals.

Acknowledgements

Without the support and help from friends and family, this book would not be in your hands now.

I would like to thank my brother Ed Baumgartner, my partner Diana Koletzki and my friend Andy Whittle for encouraging me to write this book as well as for their initial comments on the concept. Thanks also to friends Steven Mecca and Maren Baermann, and brother Phil Baumgartner for going through an early draft. Everyone's feedback resulted in substantial changes to the way this book was written.

Many thanks also to my old friend David Benson, the world's best proof-reader, for going through the final draft – during his holiday no less. I owe him big time.

Great thanks to my sons Alexander and Benjamin for believing in me and being patient while I've worked on this book.

Finally, a great big thanks to you for reading this book to the very end!

About the Author

Teacher, traveller, artist, writer, Eurocrat and entrepreneur, Jeffrey Baumgartner has led an eclectic life that has spanned three continents and included careers that have ranged from teaching English in Portugal to launching one of Thailand's first Internet and multimedia production houses; from writing magazine columns in Asia to promoting e-commerce in Europe through the European Commission.

Along the way, he has learned a great deal about how groups of people behave and, particularly, innovate. He developed this knowledge into a structured innovation process and commercialised it in 2003 by founding jpb.com, a leading innovation process management software and consultancy company with offices in the Brussels and New York City areas as well as representative offices around the world.

In addition, Jeffrey co-founded and co-manages the Brussels Imagination Club, a non-profit group devoted to experimentation in teaching and facilitation.

He has also written widely on creativity and innovation in the eJournal Report 103. His articles have been reprinted in magazines, books, theses, blogs and newsletters.

Jeffrey currently lives with his two sons and two cats in Erps-Kwerps, Belgium.

www.ingramcontent.com/pod-product-compliance
Lightning Source LLC
LaVergne TN
LVHW091127060225
803034LV00002B/176